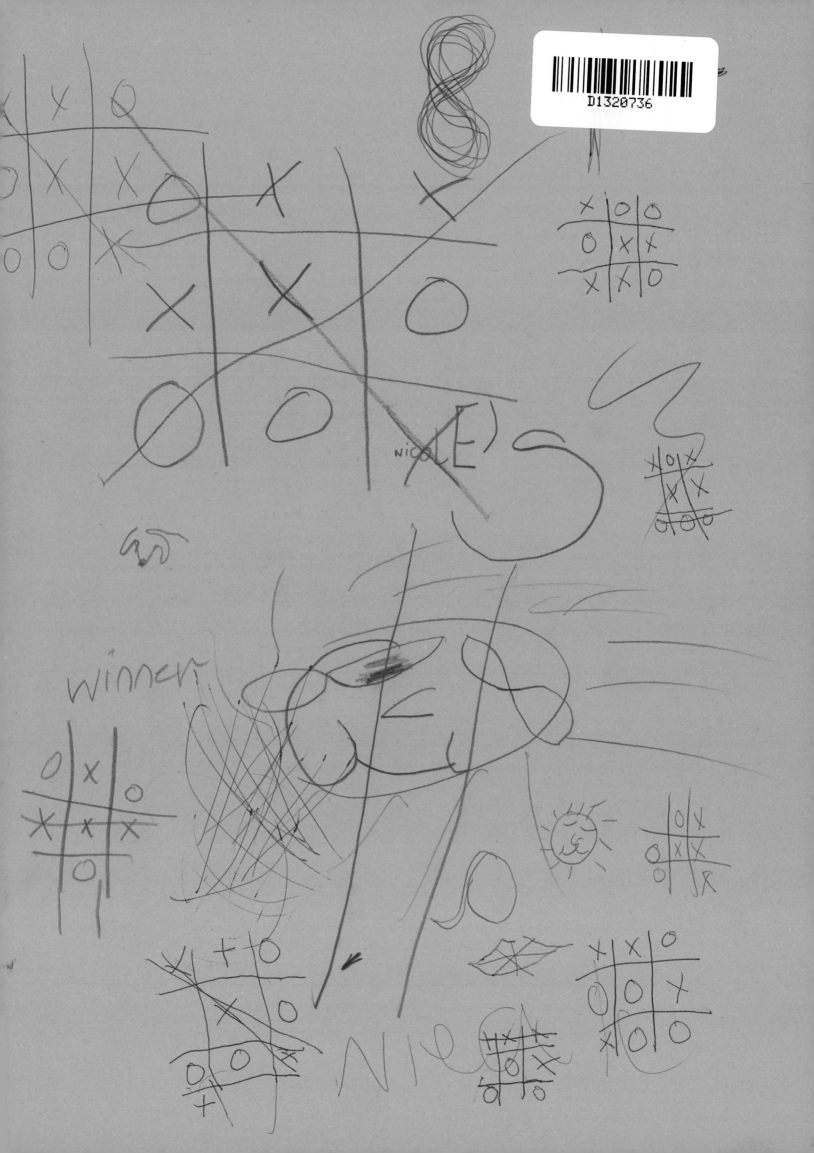

DK Guide to
MAMMALS

Ben Morgan

A Dorling Kindersley Book

LONDON, NEW YORK, MUNICH,
MELBOURNE, and DELHI

Project Editor Deborah Lock
Art Editor Jacqueline Gooden
Publishing Manager Sue Leonard
Managing Art Editor Clare Shedden
Category Publisher Mary Ling
DTP Designer Almudena Díaz
Picture Research Bridget Tily
Jacket Design Dean Price
Production Linda Dare

First published in Great Britain in 2003 by
Dorling Kindersley Limited
80 Strand, London WC2R 0RL

Penguin Group

2 4 6 8 10 9 7 5 3 1

A CIP catalogue record for this book
is available from the British Library

ISBN 0-7513-3918-0

Colour reproduction by GRB Editrice, S.r.l., Verona

Printed and bound by
Mondadori Printing S.p.A., Verona, Italy

See our complete
catalogue at
www.dk.com

CONTENTS

WHAT IS A MAMMAL?

SIXTY-FIVE MILLION YEARS AGO, a gigantic comet slammed into Earth and wrecked the planet's climate. It was a catastrophe for the dinosaurs – they were wiped out entirely – but it cleared the way for another class of animals to take over. The mammals (class Mammalia) were little more than small, nervous creatures of the night at that time, but they had already evolved some of the features that were to help them succeed, such as hair, warm blood, and milk glands. With the dinosaurs out of the way, the mammals entered a new phase in their evolution. They exploded into thousands of new forms, conquering land, sea, and air to become the biggest and most spectacular animals on Earth.

MILK AND MOTHERS
The defining feature of mammals is that they feed their young on the milk they produce. The very word mammal comes from the Latin word mamma, meaning breast. In addition, for many species, the period of parental care is a time for their young to learn vital survival skills. The cleverest mammals, such as humans and orang-utans, have the most to learn and so spend the longest with their mothers.

A VERY STRANGE MAMMAL
Humans are mammals. Our species, *Homo sapiens*, belongs to the great ape family, along with chimps, orang-utans, and gorillas. In some ways we are very peculiar mammals. Our brains are abnormally large, and we have lost most of our hair. We are the only mammal species that walks on two legs, and we are possibly the only one with a complex language.

Mammals are warm-blooded, a feature they share with birds.

Mammalian skin often has scent glands and sweat glands.

KEY FEATURES
Mammals have various unique features that set them apart from the rest of the animal kingdom. They have mammary glands that produce milk, and hair to keep them warm (though whales have lost their hair). Mammals also differ from other animals in aspects of their teeth, jawbones, ears, internal organs, and blood cells.

Legs are directly below the body to carry the weight.

SCENTS AND SMELLS

Smell is very important to mammals because most use body odours to communicate. When a rhino sprays the ground with urine, it leaves a unique scent as a message for other rhinos, telling its age, sex, social status, and whether it wants to breed.

GETTING AROUND

The first true mammals were probably four-legged animals that scuttled about like shrews. After the dinosaurs perished, the mammals diversified and found new ways of getting around. Some grew wings and took to the air. Others adapted to life in water, their limbs turning into flippers. Thousands remained four-legged, but today they vary from silent stalkers prowling along the ground to agile climbers in the treetops.

Mammals have larger brains than other animals and are cleverer.

JAGUAR

LEAF-NOSED BAT

BOTTLENOSE DOLPHIN

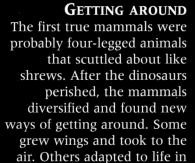

BROWN CAPUCHIN MONKEY

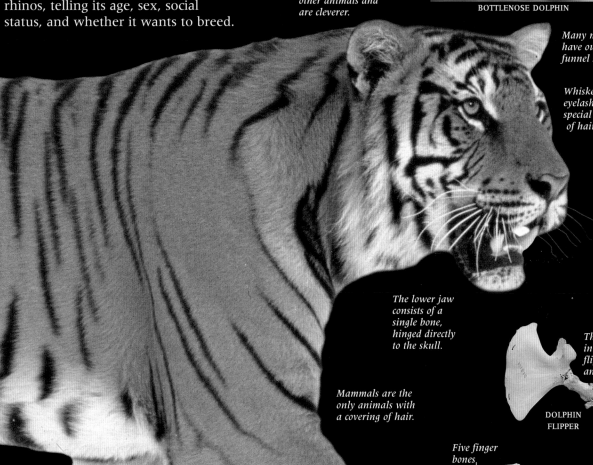

Many mammals have outer ears to funnel sound waves.

Whiskers and eyelashes are special types of hair.

Mammalian teeth mesh together precisely and come in distinct varieties, such as canines, incisors, and molars.

BAT WING

The lower jaw consists of a single bone, hinged directly to the skull.

The arm bones in a dolphin's flipper are short and stubby.

DOLPHIN FLIPPER

Mammals are the only animals with a covering of hair.

The wing of a bat is supported by extended finger bones.

Five finger bones

Forearm bones (radius and ulna)

Upper arm bone (humerus)

MONKEY ARM

Mammals have a skeletal plan with four limbs, each ending in five digits, on average.

THE BARE BONES

Mammals look very different externally, but strip away the flesh and they all have the same basic skeleton. Evolution has simply changed the size of various bones to create the diversity of shapes that exists today. Birds, reptiles, fish, and amphibians also have this kind of skeleton. Scientists call all these animals vertebrates – animals with backbones.

TEMPERATURE CONTROL

Mammals are warm-blooded (endothermic), which means their bodies generate heat from within to keep them continuously warm. In contrast, animals such as lizards and frogs are cold-blooded (ectothermic) – their body temperature goes up and down depending on outside climate conditions. Most mammals have a constant internal temperature, but this varies from species to species. Humans have a body temperature of 37°C (99°F), but rabbits and cats are warmer at 39°C (102°F), and armadillos are cooler at 32°C (90°F). Being warm-blooded allows mammals to stay active at night and survive in places where reptiles and frogs would freeze, but mammals pay a high price for their on-board heating system. To survive, they need about ten times as much food as cold-blooded animals. About 90 percent of their food is burned up just for keeping themselves warm.

COOLING OFF
Cold-blooded animals simply let their body temperature rise in hot weather, but mammals have to keep a constant temperature. Hippos cool off by wallowing in mud and water. Walruses blush to lose heat, dogs pant, and cats sweat (though only through the soles of their feet). Kangaroos lick their arms and hold them out to dry. Elephants flap their ears or hose themselves with water.

LIFE IN THE FAST LANE

Keeping warm is a problem for small mammals, like the southern flying squirrel. They lose heat faster than large mammals because the ratio between the body's surface area and volume is greater (peas get cold more quickly than potatoes for the same reason). So, to stay warm, small animals lead fast, furious lives. They spend most of their time frantically searching for food, and they grow old and die in just a few years.

Warm-blooded animals can stay active even on the coldest nights.

Sleeping bats can go into a state called torpor, letting their body temperature fall.

WARM- OR COLD-BLOODED?

Some bats are so small that they can't get enough food to keep constantly warm. Instead of wasting energy generating heat while they rest, they let their body temperature plummet to that of their surroundings. Hibernating mammals do this in winter, but certain bat species can do it every day. When they wake up, they have to exercise vigorously until they become warm enough to fly again.

FUELING THE BODY

Some cold-blooded animals can get by with only one meal a year, but mammals need to eat far more often. Carnivores, such as polar bears, get all their energy from meat, while herbivores like the proboscis monkey make do with leaves. Shrews are omnivores – they eat both animals and plant foods. All mammals have teeth and digestive systems specialized to extract as much energy as possible from their food.

The bushy tail doubles as a blanket to wrap around the body.

The snow leopard has woolly underfur up to 12 cm (5 in) thick.

FUR COATS

Fur coats are vital for keeping warm. Only the largest sea mammals do without them, but they have an insulating layer of blubber below the skin. Fur usually has two layers: an outer layer of long, bristly "guard hairs" for protection, and an inner layer of soft underfur for warmth.

REPRODUCTION

SCIENTISTS SPLIT MAMMALS into three major groups depending on how they reproduce. Monotremes are unusual mammals that lay eggs; only three species exist. Marsupials carry their babies in a pouch. Placental mammals – the most common type of mammal – carry babies inside the body, where they feed through an organ called a placenta. Some mammals produce only one baby at a time, caring for it to give it a good chance of survival. Others have lots of babies and provide them with little but milk. The majority perish, but a few make it to adulthood.

A pair of guanacos strike a dance-like pose during their courtship.

BABY FOOD

Although male mammals have nipples, only the females produce milk (with one bizarre exception: the male Dayak fruit bat). Milk is a mixture of water and nutrients, including protein, fat, carbohydrate, and vitamins. It also contains antibodies, which protect babies from disease. Its content varies enormously between species. Sea lion milk is about 50 percent fat, allowing baby sea lions to double their weight in days, but human milk is only four percent fat. Lion milk is very sugary, providing lion cubs with the instant energy they need for playing.

Lion cubs depend on their mother's milk until they are about three months old.

THE MATING GAME

The first stage of reproduction is courtship, when mammals try to attract a partner. In most species the females make the choice, so the males have to work hard to impress them. Often the males try to prove themselves by fighting rivals or winning a territory. Mating may occur at a certain time of year – the breeding season – so that young are born when food is plentiful.

Female tenrecs give birth by the dozen. The young start breeding when only a month old.

FAST BREEDERS

The common tenrec – a Madagascan animal a bit like a hedgehog – has the most nipples (29) and the largest litters (up to 32) of any mammal. In theory, a single tenrec could produce a population of millions in one year if all its offspring bred at the maximum rate.

Baby gorillas develop inside the mother for about nine months – the same as humans.

PLACENTAL MAMMALS

Placental mammals give their young a head start in life by letting them develop to an advanced stage in the mother's body. Baby elephants spend 20 months inside the mother, and are born so well-developed that they can run within minutes of birth. Before birth, placental mammals are nourished by a placenta, a complex organ in which the baby's blood and the mother's blood flow past each other without mixing.

MONOTREMES

Echidnas and platypuses are the only mammals that lay eggs. Echidnas carry their eggs in a pouch, but the platypus puts them in a nest. Monotremes have no nipples – the mother's milk oozes into her fur like sweat.

Echidnas have spiny bodies like hedgehogs.

MARSUPIALS

Marsupials give birth to wormlike babies far tinier than the young of placental mammals. Newborn kangaroos are the size of beans and don't even have hind legs. After birth, they wriggle through the mother's fur and into a pouch, where they stay for up to a year. A young kangaroo is called a joey.

GROWING UP

Female elephants suckle their young with a pair of breasts between the front legs.

MOST ANIMALS SIMPLY ABANDON THEIR YOUNG to fate after giving birth or laying eggs, but mammals are different. Mammals feed and care for their offspring during the perilous early days of life. This period of parental care frees the young from the need to fend for themselves and gives them time to learn valuable survival skills. Baby turtles rely on instinct alone when they hatch, but mammals are free to play, explore, and copy their parents – all vital parts of the learning process. Parental care, coupled with large brains, is one of the features that makes mammals so successful and adaptable. It is most important in primates and especially so in humans – we have the longest childhood of any animal.

CHANGING SHAPE

A fox cub is born helpless and blind, but it grows quickly on its mother's milk and soon starts to change shape. By two weeks, its eyes are open, and at four weeks, it starts to leave the den and explore. Its snout, ears, and legs get steadily longer, and the rolls of insulating puppy fat on its body gradually disappear.

By ten weeks, a fox cub has developed its adult colours.

NEWBORN   2 WEEKS   4 WEEKS   8 WEEKS   10 WEEKS
FOX CUB

HITCHING A RIDE

Baby anteaters spend their first year or so riding on their mother's back. This is especially important for tree-dwelling anteaters, such as tamanduas, which live in the forests of South and Central America. The mother tamandua provides a safe perch for her baby until it is old enough to risk climbing on its own.

Tamandua's raid treetop ants' nests and eat up to 9,000 ants a day.

PROTECTIVE PARENTS

An elephant takes about 17 years to grow up. The calf and mother form a very strong bond and spend the first ten years close together, using their trunks to maintain physical contact. Elephants live in all-female herds and are fiercely protective of all the young in the herd, not just their own. If a person or animal gets too close, the leader of the herd spreads her ears and charges while bellowing thunderously through her trunk.

KILLER INSTINCTS

Cats sometimes give their youngsters live prey to play with. Though it seems cruel to us, this is an important way to develop the skills they need to hunt. Cheetah cubs practise killing baby gazelles, learning how to trip them up as they try to race away.

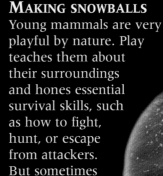

WATCH WITH MOTHER

Cracking open a nut with rocks is one of the trickiest skills for a chimpanzee to master. Young chimps spend years watching their mothers doing it and slowly acquire the skill themselves by patient trial and error.

MAKING SNOWBALLS

Young mammals are very playful by nature. Play teaches them about their surroundings and hones essential survival skills, such as how to fight, hunt, or escape from attackers. But sometimes mammals seem to play just for the fun of it.

In winter, Japanese macaques make large snowballs by rolling them along the ground, in the same way as children make heads for snowmen.

Young elephants hide under their mother's legs for protection.

PRIMITIVE PRIMATES

Grasping hands, large brains, and forward-facing eyes are the hallmarks of primates – the branch of the mammal family tree to which our own species belongs. Primates live throughout the world's tropical forests, and most are tree-dwellers. Apes and monkeys are the most famous primates, but there are many other, smaller species that are less well known. While apes and monkeys tend to be active by day, their smaller cousins are mostly secretive animals of the night, with big eyes for seeing in the dark and long, moist snouts for smelling their way around. Scientists call these mammals the prosimians, or primitive primates.

TWIGGY FINGER
The aye aye is a type of lemur with a middle finger that looks like a dead twig. After gnawing a hole in a tree trunk, the aye aye pokes in its finger and hooks beetle grubs on a sharp claw. This unique finger also makes a handy scoop for reaching into coconuts and eggs.

LEAPING LEMURS
The island of Madagascar near Africa is home to a group of primates found nowhere else: the lemurs. The sifaka is a type of lemur that moves about by leaping. It jumps from trees and lands upright on vertical boughs, which it grabs with colossal thumbs on its feet. Its arms are so short that when on the ground it has to bounce as if on a trampoline with its arms held high for balance.

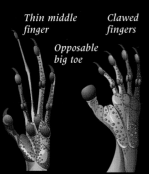

Thin middle finger

Clawed fingers

Opposable big toe

Rounded pads on fingertips

Grooming claw

AYE AYE HAND   AYE AYE FOOT   TARSIER HAND   TARSIER FOOT

HANDS AND FEET

The hands and feet of primitive primates remind us of our own. They have opposable thumbs and opposable big toes – these move the opposite way to the rest and so allow primates to grip branches as they climb. Primates tend to have nails rather than claws, giving improved grip and touch. For extra grip, tarsiers have huge round fingertip pads.

3-D VISION

The eyes of primates both face forward – quite unlike the sideways-facing eyes of rabbits or deer, for instance. Forward-facing eyes see the world twice, but they create two slightly different pictures. By combining these images, the primate brain produces a single, 3-D image of the world. Seeing in 3-D allows primates to judge distances.

The lorises of Asia have especially big eyes for seeing in the dark.

BOUNCING BABIES

The bushbabies of Africa can cover great distances in seconds by making a quick succession of leaps. Rather like sifakas, they use massive hind legs to spring from trees and then hold their bodies upright as they fly and land. These tiny nocturnal animals have astonishingly quick reflexes, and can even snatch passing moths from the air in mid-leap.

To mark their territory, bushbabies urinate on their feet and leave a trail of smelly footprints.

Ring-tailed lemurs like to sunbathe. They bask in sunlight sitting down, with their arms spread out.

STINK FIGHTS

Most primitive primates are nocturnal loners, but ring-tailed lemurs live in large groups and are active during the day. When rival groups clash, they have a "stink fight". The males rub their tails between scent glands on their wrists and then march towards each other, flicking their tails angrily to waft the scent. This battle of odours allows them to settle their differences without coming to blows.

MONKEY BUSINESS

FEW ANIMALS ARE AS ENTERTAINING OR CLEVER as nature's greatest acrobats: the monkeys. These agile climbers live throughout the tropics, mostly in forests. Unlike the shy nocturnal primates, they form lively social groups and are active by day in a world of noise and colour. Colour vision is their top sense, helping them spot ripe fruit and leaves at a glance. Monkeys are intelligent and adaptable. Their big brains not only help them find food – they are vital for understanding the web of relationships in monkey society.

DAWN CHORUS

Whenever the sun rises or sets in the forests of South and Central America, howler monkeys begin their deafening chorus. Their roars are among the loudest made by any land animal and can be heard many miles away. The chorus has the same purpose as a wolf's howl – it tells neighbouring monkeys to keep out of the group's territory.

Tamarins have extravagant hairstyles that range from fiery manes to white mohicans.

MINIATURE MONKEYS

Tamarins are tiny monkeys that flit about the treetops of Brazil, twittering nervously as they scamper along the thinnest twigs looking for insects and fruit. Tamarins always give birth to twins. The babies ride on the adults' backs but keep hopping from one adult to another. Sometimes they all crowd together on their favourite carer.

The tail can even pick up food.

The "hand" on the tail has a patch of bare, gripping skin, complete with sweat glands, a sense of touch, and fingerprint patterns.

FINDING FOOD

South American squirrel monkeys are constantly on the lookout for new sources of food. These clever and resourceful animals eat everything from flowers and fruits to insects and spiders, and they sometimes follow larger monkeys around to pilfer leftovers. Like nearly all monkeys, they use their dexterous hands and good eyesight to inspect everything they eat.

A HANDY TAIL

Spider monkeys of South America are so named because their tails work as fifth limbs, making them look like giant spiders as they clamber among the branches. Spider monkeys can swing under branches as gibbons can, using their thumbless hands as hooks.

OUT OF THE WOODS

Most monkeys are tree dwellers, but some have adapted to life on the ground. Baboons made the transition around the same time that our ancestors did, when Africa's rainforests began turning into grasslands. Like humans, they adapted to grassland life by learning to hunt. Though they mostly eat grass and plant roots, foraging with hands just like ours, they also kill and eat young gazelles.

SOCIAL GLUE

Hamadryas baboons live in vast troops of up to 1,000. The glue that holds them together is grooming – like all monkeys, they spends hours stroking and combing each other's fur. Grooming triggers the release of brain chemicals called endorphins, inducing a kind of relaxing high. Sometimes monkeys get so relaxed during grooming that they topple over and flake out.

THE APES

PEOPLE TEND TO CONFUSE APES with monkeys, but there are important differences. Apes are more upright and have no tails. They climb in a different way, using their huge arms to haul themselves up trees and hang from branches. Apes have bigger brains and are cleverer. They can manipulate and deceive each other, recognize themselves in mirrors, and learn to use all sorts of tools.

BEG FOR FOOD

INTENSE FEAR OR EXCITEMENT

FEAR GRIN

CONTEMPLATING

MAKING FACES

Although none of the apes has language anything like as complex as ours, they can communicate in sophisticated ways. Africa's chimps make at least 30 different calls and sometimes kick the giant roots of rainforest trees to make booming noises that carry far away. They also communicate with facial expressions more varied than any other animal's. Some are the opposite of our own – for instance, baring the teeth in a grin is a sign of fear to a chimp.

GENTLE GIANTS

Gorillas are the biggest primates and can weigh up to 210 kg (33 stone). Despite their great bulk and fearsome image, they are placid herbivores that spend all day chomping leaves in the mountains and rainforests of Central Africa. They move about as they forage, taking only a few leaves from each plant so as not to destroy their food supply.

CHIMP TOOL KITS

The ability of chimps to use tools is a reminder that these clever apes are our close cousins. They use sticks to fish for termites, rocks to crack open nuts, leaves as sponges and tissues, and all sorts of plants as herbal medicines. One captive chimp even learned how to light a barbecue and cook his own sausages.

All large apes walk on the soles of their hind feet and the knuckles of their hands.

Gorilla social groups are dominated by huge, silvery haired males called silverbacks, which mate with all the females.

SINGING SWINGERS

Gibbons swing through trees with breathtaking agility, using their hands as hooks. Their wrists and shoulders are so flexible that they can turn through 360 degrees, while hanging from one hand. Males and females live in monogamous pairs, like humans. Some species sing haunting duets to declare their bond.

GROWING UP SLOWLY

Young orang-utans spend up to ten years with their mothers. Like other apes, they grow up slowly as they need to learn many complex skills to survive. These gentle animals live in the steamy rainforests of Borneo and Sumatra and are threatened by deforestation.

BRAIN POWER

THERE IS A GOOD REASON why mammals make the best pets – they are cleverer than other animals. While pet snakes and birds have to be caged for their own good, cats and dogs are smart enough to wander freely. Mammals, in general, have larger brains than other animals (though there are several small-brained exceptions). They have sharper memories, are quicker to learn, and can adapt their behaviour to new situations. The cleverest mammals even show hints of abilities once thought to be uniquely human, including tool use and the beginnings of language.

LEARNING THE ROPES
As anyone with a birdfeeder knows, squirrels are ingenious as well as acrobatic. They can get past almost any obstacle in their quest for food, even if it means scurrying along a clothes-line upside down. They also have amazing memory skills. In autumn, grey squirrels hoard thousands of nuts for the winter, burying each one individually and memorizing its location.

FINDING THE WAY
Like many mammals, rats find their way about by memorizing the position of landmarks. They are so good at this that they can quickly learn the route through a maze and remember it perfectly. In the wild, rats use smell as well as vision to build up a map of landmarks. Their regular foraging routes become so ingrained that a rat will continue to leap over a remembered obstacle even after it has been removed.

BRAINY DOLPHINS
Dolphins have brains almost as large and complex as ours, but scientists are not sure what they use them for. With no hands, dolphins can't make tools, though they sometimes pick up sponges to protect their noses while foraging. Dolphins whistle and click to each other, but do their calls mean that they have a language? Captive dolphins can learn to understand sign language, and wild dolphins have personalized whistles that they use as names. But as yet there is no clear evidence that dolphins can string sounds together into sentences – an essential feature of human language.

The diet of a sea otter includes clams, sea urchins, crabs, and abalone from the sea bed.

TOOL USERS

Using tools was once thought to be the sole preserve of our own species, but we now know that many other animals are tool-users. The sea otter uses a rock as an anvil. It dives to the sea bed for shellfish and returns to the surface to eat them. Floating on its back, it places the rock on its belly and smashes the shellfish against it to break them open.

TOOL MAKERS

Orang-utans and chimpanzees not only use tools, but make them too. Both use specially prepared twigs to "fish" for ants and termites, and both are expert nest-makers, building a treetop sleeping platform every night by folding branches together. If it's raining, orang-utans add a roof to their nest or use giant leaves as umbrellas.

TALKING APES

Apes will never be able to speak to us because their voice boxes can't produce human sounds, but could they talk in other ways? Scientists have tried teaching our closest relatives – chimpanzees and bonobos – to communicate with sign language and symbols. So far, the most successful ape was a young bonobo called Kanzi, who picked up several hundred "words" by watching his adoptive mother being trained to use symbols. Kanzi went on to construct his own short sentences, but he only progressed to a two-year-old child's level.

Kanzi the bonobo talks to his trainer by pointing at symbols on a chart.

Bottlenose dolphins are curious and playful animals. They sometimes play with human divers or leap out of the water for fun.

ON THE HOOF

A HOOF IS NOTHING MORE THAN A TOENAIL, though a very big one. Long ago, the ancestors of hoofed mammals had feet much like ours. Over time, nails evolved into hooves, the heel travelled halfway up the leg, and these animals ended up walking gracefully on their toe tips. In some species, all but the middle toe withered away. The changes gave hoofed mammals a vital ability – speed, which was essential for running from meat eaters. Today, these endurance runners make up one of the biggest and most successful groups of mammals on Earth.

BATTLING MALES

Hoofed mammals are mostly plant eaters, but they can be just as violent and aggressive as any meat eater. Battles between males are common, especially when the prize is the right to mate with a whole herd of females. African plains zebras live in harems – groups of females owned by a single stallion. In the breeding season, the male faces challenges from rivals determined to steal his harem. The frenzy of bites and kicks can leave either contender mortally wounded.

With their lips drawn back, fighting zebras tear at each other with their teeth.

PLANT EATERS

Most hoofed mammals are either grazers or browsers. Grazers eat low plants like grass, while browsers nibble trees and shrubs, often specializing in food at a particular height. Gerenuks can stand on their hind legs to reach higher than most antelopes, though they are no match for giraffes.

BIRTH ON THE HOOF

A dangerous moment in a wildebeest's life comes immediately after birth, when the youngster is easy prey for predators. However, newborns can stagger to their feet within minutes of birth and can run with the herd within an hour. For added safety, all the females in a herd give birth during the same three-week period, ensuring there are far too many babies for the predators to kill.

The mother gives birth standing up. She eats the afterbirth and licks the baby to rouse it. During this critically dangerous period, wildebeest mothers are fiercely protective and will charge angrily at any curious onlookers.

A mouthful of grass takes about 80 hours to pass through the body of a ruminant, such as this highland cow.

ODD AND EVEN

Scientists split the hoofed mammals into two major groups, depending on whether they have an odd or even number of toes. In odd-toed animals, such as rhinos and horses, the weight rests on the central or single toe. In even-toed animals, such as camels, a pair of toes carries most of the weight.

HORSE   CAMEL   RHINOCEROS

CHEWING THE CUD

Plant food is difficult to digest, so some hoofed mammals eat it twice. The first time they swallow a mouthful of grass, it goes into a special stomach chamber called a rumen. Later, the animal regurgitates the partly-digested grass, or cud, for a second chewing and swallows it again. This type of digestion, called rumination, is slow but efficient.

The ridges on horns prevent them from slipping in a sparring match.

The impala is one of the most common grazing animals in Africa. Only the male has horns.

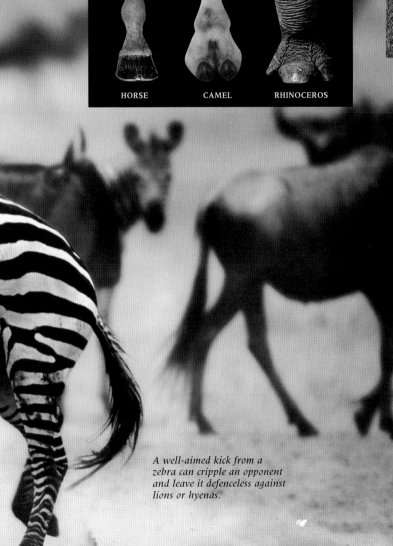
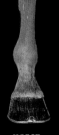

A well-aimed kick from a zebra can cripple an opponent and leave it defenceless against lions or hyenas.

HORNS AND ANTLERS

Horns or antlers allow hoofed mammals to settle disputes without resorting to bloodshed. By locking their horns or antlers together and pushing (sparring), a pair can quickly work out who is strongest, while preventing injury.

Long necks allow giraffes to reach the parts of trees that other animals can't.

LAND GIANTS

FOR SOME MAMMALS, the best form of self defence is size. Elephants, rhinos, giraffes, and hippos are simply too big to attack, even for a whole pride of lions – though cunning predators can sometimes fatally trip giraffes by chasing them over rocky ground. The young of these giant herbivores are much more vulnerable, but their parents are very protective. In Africa, charging elephants, rhinos, and hippos gore hundreds of people to death every year, usually to protect their young.

GIRAFFE

The prize for the tallest living animal goes to the giraffe, which can reach 6 m (20 ft) tall. Giraffes have such long necks and legs that they appear to move in slow motion when they gallop.

HIPPO

With water to support their bulk and keep them cool, hippos spend the heat of the day resting in lakes and rivers, where they defecate continually to mark their territory. At night, they come onto land to eat grass.

AFRICAN ELEPHANT

The male African elephant is the biggest land animal on Earth, weighing up to about 6 tonnes. The largest elephant on record was a bull elephant from Angola, which was shot by a hunter in 1955. It stood 4 m (13 ft) tall and weighed a staggering 11 tonnes (12 tons) – as heavy as 150 men.

Wild elephants live in herds ruled by females. The huge adult males lead mostly solitary lives.

THE BIG FIVE

By weight, the top five biggest land animals are adult males of the species shown on the right. Males are usually bigger than females because they have to fight each other to win mates. Even the lightest of these animals – the giraffe – weighs as much as 30 men.

GIRAFFE

AFRICAN ELEPHANT

ASIAN ELEPHANT

WHITE RHINOCEROS

HIPPOPOTAMUS

5.4 TONNES (6 TONS)

6 TONNES (6.6 TONS)

2 TONNES (2.2 TONS)

2.3 TONNES (2.5 TONS)

3.2 TONNES (3.5 TONS)

BLACK RHINO

Charging rhinos are not just terrifying – they are faster than Olympic sprinters and surprisingly nimble. Yet speed and strength are no match for bullets, and rhinos are so short-sighted that poachers can walk right up to them without being seen. Fewer than 3,000 black rhinos are left on Earth. As the species gets rarer, the precious horns fetch ever greater sums of money for making them into Chinese medicines and Arabian dagger handles.

WHITE RHINO

White rhinos and black rhinos are both actually grey. The name "white rhino" comes from the Afrikaans word *weit*, which means wide. White rhinos have wide lips for eating grass, while black rhinos have hooked lips for eating twigs.

INCREDIBLE JOURNEYS

L OST DOGS ARE WELL KNOWN FOR THEIR UNCANNY KNACK of finding the way home from miles away. Their instinctive ability to navigate is a talent shared by the mammal world's great travellers. Wild dogs and oryxes, for instance, are restless nomads that spend their lives constantly searching for food. Reindeer and wildebeest travel with the seasons, embarking on epic voyages called migrations. Their herds seem to have a collective wisdom that tells them when and where to go. Exactly how travelling mammals find the way is something of a mystery. Perhaps they follow the Sun and stars, magnetic fields, or distant smells and landmarks.

On their journey, reindeer feed on lichen buried under the snow.

CIRCLING THE SERENGETI

Earth's greatest wildlife spectacle happens in the Serengeti grasslands of east Africa, where up to two million wildebeest migrate in a great circle each year, following seasonal rains in search of fresh grazing. Their perilous journey takes them through crocodile-infested rivers, where many are crushed in the panic to cross.

During the Serengeti migration, crocodiles cluster around crossing sites in the Mara River. With only their eyes above the water, they sneak close to the wildebeest and wait for the right moment to make a sudden lunge.

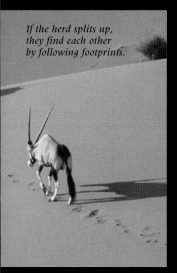

If the herd splits up, they find each other by following footprints.

DESERT NOMADS

Arabian oryxes wander endlessly looking for plants to eat, trekking up to 30 km (19 miles) every night, when the heat is less stifling. Wild oryxes were hunted to extinction in the 1970s, but a few survived in zoos. In the 1980s, scientists released captive animals back to the desert, and there are now a few hundred surviving in the wild.

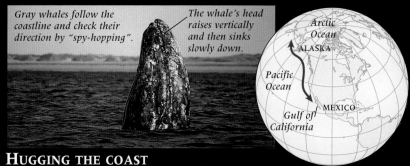

Gray whales follow the coastline and check their direction by "spy-hopping".

The whale's head raises vertically and then sinks slowly down.

HUGGING THE COAST

Every spring, gray whales set off on the longest migration of any mammal. They leave their winter breeding areas in the subtropical waters of Baja in Mexico, which are ideal for young calves who don't have enough blubber to cope with cold water. They swim 10,000 km (6,000 miles) north to the Arctic Ocean to reach their summer feeding grounds, and stay until the water freezes over.

ARCTIC EXPLORERS

Reindeer (called caribou in North America) have migrated north with the Arctic summer for thousands of years, but these days the herds are often accompanied by Arctic people, such as the Sami of Scandinavia and Russia. The Sami own the herds and lead them with sleds, but the reindeer are really just doing what comes naturally. Reindeer are the only deer in which both sexes have antlers. They also have deeply divided hooves that spread like snowshoes.

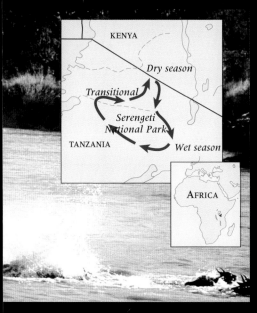

ON THE RUN

For African wild dogs, hunting is all about travelling. A pack covers huge distances every day and needs a territory of up to 2,000 sq km (770 sq miles) to meet its needs. Wild dogs wear out large animals by chasing them to exhaustion, snapping at the animal's belly whenever it slows.

CAT FAMILY

Cats are nature's most specialized carnivores, built to live on a diet consisting mostly of meat. All 37 species are ruthless killing machines, bristling with natural weapons and programmed by instinct to hunt with stealth and cunning. Domestic cats and their wild cousins have more in common than you might suppose. They share the same retractable claws, night vision, and vicious canine teeth. Like domestic cats, wild cats can pounce silently, land on four feet when they fall, and purr when content.

CLAWS FOR CLIMBING

Like nearly all cats, leopards have razor-sharp claws that serve both as weapons and as hooks for climbing. To keep them sharp, they are withdrawn into sheaths. Most cats live in forests and are good climbers, though up is easier than down! Patterned coats camouflage them in the dappled forest light.

A POWERFUL BUILD

Cats are ambush predators, built to stalk in silence and then attack with a burst of power. Unlike dogs, which are tall and athletic for long-distance running, cats have a sturdier, more powerful frame, yet they are also lithe and agile. Their muscular legs are built for pouncing and climbing. Their snouts are shorter than dogs', and their jaws are massive to accommodate muscles that inflict a fatal bite.

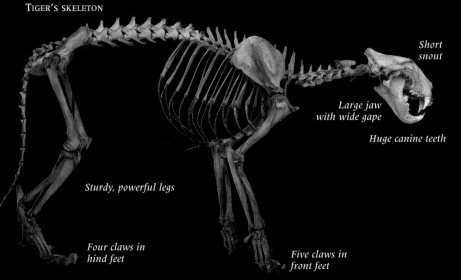

TIGER'S SKELETON

Short snout

Large jaw with wide gape

Huge canine teeth

Long tail for balance

Sturdy, powerful legs

Four claws in hind feet

Five claws in front feet

A typical cat's litter has two to three infants.

BABY CARE

Female cats are attentive mothers. They will hide their young in a den while away and call to greet them on returning. If the den proves unsafe, the mother quickly finds a new site and carries the infants there, one by one, by the scruff of the neck.

NIGHT VISION

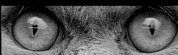
DAY VISION

A lion's eyes glow at night because they contain a reflective layer called a tapetum.

NIGHT VISION

Cats are creatures of the night. Though they can't see as much colour as we can, their eyes are six times more sensitive in the dark. To catch as much light as possible, their eyes contain a reflective layer at the back. Depending on the species, cats' pupils shrink to dots or slits in daylight, but open to huge black discs at night.

A lion cub becomes limp when picked up by the neck.

SOCIABLE CATS

Cats are renowned for being loners, but some are more friendly than others. Male cheetahs often form small groups, probably because this helps them to take over other cheetahs' territories. Lions live in large groups called prides, and even stray domestic cats can be sociable. They sometimes rear their young in communal dens, the mothers taking turns to suckle all the young at once.

All cats have rough tongues to clean their fur and keep it fluffy. Grooming also serves to strengthen social bonds.

POUNCING PUMA

Cats are agile pouncers, able to spring off their haunches and sail gracefully through the air. Pouncing is handy for surprising prey or for jumping up trees. Domestic cats can slip up fences with gravity-defying ease.

SOFT LANDING

A superb sense of balance allows cats to land on all fours when they fall. First the neck twists until the head is level. Then the rest of the body swings quickly around. The front legs stretch out and absorb the impact of landing.

The head twists around first.

The rest of the body quickly follows.

The front legs touch down before the back legs.

27

KILLER CATS

A HUNTING WAY OF LIFE not only requires great strength and killer weapons, but also cunning, practice, and adaptability. The typical cat hunts alone and at night, using a mixture of stealth and patience to sneak up on victims. Cats are fascinated by their prey and spend many hours watching them, looking for weaknesses. Cats also hunt and kill for fun, while honing their skills. As they grow up, most cats become expert at catching particular types of animals, but they are all opportunists, killing whatever they can eat – including humans.

THE STALK
For most cats, the hunt begins with a stalk. The aim is to creep close enough to the prey to launch a surprise attack. Tigers use the cover of long grass to camouflage their approach. With eyes locked on the target, they inch forward only when the prey looks away. Silent footwork is crucial, so they feel the ground with their paws before shifting their weight. Soft pads on the paws muffle the footsteps.

THE POUNCE
A stalk generally ends with a pounce. Guided by hearing alone, a serval can sail 4 m (13 ft) through the air to land precisely on its prey's back. The force of the landing often smashes the victim's spine.

ARMED TO THE TEETH
Huge canine teeth are not for butchering meat – they are for capturing and killing. Most cats immobilize their prey with a suffocating bite to the throat. With a lion's canines deeply embedded in the neck, only the strongest victim has any hope of struggling free. If the prey is small, a skilful bite will dislocate its backbone. This severs the spinal cord, paralysing the prey's body immediately.

LAND SPEED RECORD

Unusually for a cat, the cheetah relies on a high-speed chase to catch its prey. It is the fastest animal on land, capable of reaching 105 kph (65 mph) as it sprints after fast-running gazelles. It brings them down by flicking the hind legs and making them stumble.

Cheetahs can sprint at full tilt for only about 20 seconds before they risk overheating.

HIDING MEALS

For leopards, catching prey is only half the battle. To protect their prize from thieving lions and hyenas, leopards face the exhausting challenge of hauling their kill up a tree. Once the prey is safely stashed, the leopard can feed at leisure over several days.

A bobcat deftly catching a muskrat.

REFLEX ACTION

Lightning reactions are vital for catching small, quick-witted prey. Bobcats make light work of catching muskrats, hares, and rabbits as they bound across snow. Their strategy is simple: knock the animal off its feet to gain the advantage; then grip it securely by hooking claws into the skin.

TEAMWORK

Lions use teamwork to bring down prey that is much larger than themselves. By working together, they can overpower full-grown wildebeest, zebras, or buffalos. Often during the hunt, they spread out, encircling the prey to block escape routes. As soon as one member of the pride has got hold of a victim's neck, the others leap on its back and use their weight to bring the animal down.

BEAR NECESSITIES

BEARS MAKE UP A TINY BRANCH OF THE MAMMAL FAMILY TREE, with only eight species, but what they lack in numbers they make up for in size and personality. They have the intelligence and curiosity of dogs, but also immensely powerful bodies. The bears in the furthest north grow to massive proportions as they fatten up for the winter hibernation, which can last more than half a year. In some ways, bears are like us. They can stand on their hind legs, climb trees (albeit clumsily), and most are omnivores – they eat plants as well as animals.

A VARIED DIET

Grizzly bears eat anything and everything, including grass, leaves, roots, berries, nuts, honey, insects, fish, clams, mice, squirrels, sheep, and even moose. Finding such varied fare requires an inquisitive mind and a good memory. Grizzlies have a mental map of their large home range and seem to know exactly where to find the best pickings at different times of the year.

BERRIES

HONEY

Sugary food like berries and honey help grizzlies fatten up for winter. They are one of the only mammal species that can last more than six months without food.

BEAR BODIES

Bears have a heavy, rounded build, with stout legs, and almost no tail. Their snouts are long and doglike, and their sense of smell is superb. Although they eat lots of plant matter, most bears are not good at digesting it – sometimes their droppings contain berries that look freshly picked.

TEETH

Bears have huge canines, but fewer sharp teeth than cats or dogs.

The sun bear of Southeast Asia uses an unusually long tongue to lick honey and insects out of holes in trees. It also has very long claws for climbing.

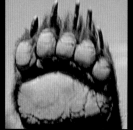

PAW

Each foot has five claws, used for digging, climbing, and tearing food.

BAMBOO BEAR

Giant pandas' diet is mainly bamboo – a type of giant grass. Bamboo forests take 30–60 years to grow, after which all the plants flower together and die. In the past, pandas coped with this by moving home, but today they are prisoners in China's few remaining patches of forest. In 1974, nearly 200 pandas died in the Wangland reserve after the bamboos flowered.

KING OF THE ICE

The biggest and most deadly bear is the polar bear, which lives exclusively on flesh – including, on rare occasions, the flesh of humans. Polar bears are sea dwellers. They roam across the frozen surface of the Arctic Ocean, stalking seals and walruses. They are confident swimmers and can paddle for miles through the icy water.

WHITE-WATER FISHING

During the salmon season in Alaska, grizzlies wade into rivers and catch migrating salmon as they leap over the foaming rapids. Some bears simply open their mouths and let the salmon jump in. Others use a deft swipe of the paw to flick the fish out of the water. During this glut of food, a grizzly might consume 40 kg (90 lbs) of fish a day, often eating only the brains and eggs and discarding the rest.

DOG FAMILY

DOMESTIC DOGS MAY BE MAN'S BEST FRIENDS, but wild members of this family of mammals are brutal carnivores. Dogs, foxes, and jackals are also highly intelligent and adaptable, able to live in groups or adapt to life on their own. Many are pack-hunters, with social lives dominated by a rigid code of conduct and a strict hierarchy. Others are more solitary, using sharp senses and cunning to catch whatever they can.

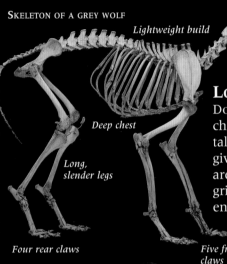

SKELETON OF A GREY WOLF

Lightweight build

Long snout

Piercing canine teeth

Deep chest

Long, slender legs

Four rear claws

Five front claws

LONG-DISTANCE RUNNERS

Dogs are natural athletes, built to chase prey to exhaustion. They have tall, slender legs and run on their toes, giving a long stride length. Their claws are blunt and nonretractable for a firm grip. The deep chest and large lungs ensure they don't get out of breath.

Dogs can tell the strength of their rivals and the size of the pack from the volume and depth of the howls.

SHARP SENSES

Hunting requires sharp senses. Most dogs have a sense of smell up to a million times more sensitive than our own. The bat-eared fox of Africa complements its sensitive nose with huge, swivelling ears that can pick up the rustle of termites and dung beetles underground.

HUNTERS AND SCAVENGERS

Dogs are supreme opportunists, switching from hunting to scavenging when the need arises. In Africa, black-backed jackals feed on the leftovers of lion and cheetah kills, even if it means fighting through a group of vultures. They will also risk their lives to snatch morsels from lions that are still feeding.

HOWLING COYOTE

The mournful howls of a coyote are a warning: they tell rivals to keep their distance. However, if the rivals aren't impressed, the howler risks inviting an attack. A safer technique is to spray smelly urine around the edge of the territory.

During the chase, the dogs snap at the victim's belly to disembowel and weaken it.

FEEDING FRENZY

By working together, African hunting dogs can bring down prey up to ten times their own size. Like wolves, they use different strategies for different prey. Small animals like antelope are torn apart in a frenzy of excitement the moment they are caught. Larger prey like wildebeest are chased to exhaustion. They don't wait for their victim to die before eating – they start feasting as soon as it collapses.

BODY LANGUAGE

Facial expressions and body language play a vital part in the social interaction between grey wolves. Their packs have a strict hierarchy, ruled by a dominant male and female – the only pair allowed to breed. The breeding pair leads the pack and makes decisions. They use a range of dominant postures and expressions to stay in charge. Lower-ranking dogs show their obedience by crouching, holding their tails between their legs, or rolling on to their backs.

With its teeth bared, ears flat, and head down, this grey wolf is signalling both defensiveness and aggression.

Grey wolves are the largest wild dogs, and are up to twice the size of domestic Alsatians.

SOCIAL LIVES

FOR MANY MAMMALS, life is easier if they gang together. Living in a social group is often a good form of defence – predators find it very difficult to sneak up unseen when there are dozens of eyes on the lookout for danger. Pack hunters, like dogs, hyenas, and lions, can take on bigger prey by pooling their strength and working as a team. They also find it easier to steal from rivals, defend their territory, and raise and protect their young. Some mammals have very fluid social groups that split up easily, but other groups are more tight-knit. Often the core of the group consists of closely related females, who stick together for life. Sometimes, completely unrelated species form a partnership, such as coyotes and American badgers, who team up to dig prairie dogs out of their burrows.

Musk oxen have the longest fur of any animal.

SAFETY IN NUMBERS

Small herbivores usually bolt at the first sign of danger, but bigger animals tend to stand their ground. When musk oxen face attack from wolves or polar bears, they draw together in a tight circle, with the youngsters in the middle behind a formidable wall of horns. Musk oxen live in northern Canada, where they have to brave subzero temperatures and ferocious winds.

FEMALES RULE

Spotted hyenas live in a society dominated by a strict female hierarchy. Even the highest-ranking male has a lower status than the lowest female. Hyena clans cooperate to defend a collective territory, though clan members frequently break up into smaller groups to hunt. At night, they communicate by making blood-curdling "woo-up" calls and cackling – hence the nickname "laughing hyenas".

Spotted hyenas raise their young in communal dens. The youngsters learn their place in the pecking order by fighting with each other from the moment they are born.

Meerkats watch for danger by standing on their hind legs, often on the top of a termite mound or a bush.

PACK HUNTERS
Dolphins live in groups called pods and have a very fluid society, with members leaving and joining all the time. Sometimes pods aggregate in groups of several hundred to cooperate in the hunting of shoaling fish, such as anchovy. By circling the fish and swimming below them, the dolphins drive them into an ever tighter formation and force them to the surface, making them easy to snatch.

Like many social animals, coatis cement the bonds between them by grooming each other.

SEPARATE SEXES
Scientists once thought that male and female coatis were different species. The large males are solitary, but the smaller females live in tight-knit groups. They tolerate the presence of males only in the breeding season and banish them afterwards.

MEERKATS UNITED
Meerkats take turns to keep a lookout while most of the group snuffle about on the ground for grubs. If the sentry sees an eagle, it makes an alarm call that sends the group sprinting in terror for the nearest hole. If the predator is a land animal, a different kind of call sends the meerkats dashing less urgently into any available hiding place.

SMALL AND WILY

T HE WORD "CARNIVORE" CONJURES UP IMAGES of lions
and tigers, but most of the 230 or so species in the
carnivore branch of the mammal family tree (the order
Carnivora) are small, wily animals like weasels, skunks,
mongooses, and raccoons. These tiny terrors make up for
their small size with cunning, agility, and determination.
They are clever enough to outsmart prey ten times their
size and swift enough to disarm animals as dangerous as
cobras. Many of the small carnivores have a lithe and
slender build for darting up and down trees or slipping
through the narrowest of spaces in their relentless pursuit
of prey. The least weasel – the smallest carnivore of all –
can even chase mice and voles deep into their burrows.

PORCUPINE KILLER
The fisher of North America is one of the only
predators that can kill a porcupine. It attacks
from the front, delivering a series of deep bites
to the porcupine's face. Each time the porcupine
turns around to present its quills, the fisher
darts around it like lightning and strikes the
face again. After about half an hour, the
wounded porcupine collapses from
exhaustion and the fisher begins
feasting on its unprotected belly.

*Wolverines have amazingly
powerful jaws to break spines
and crunch frozen meat.
Their wide feet act like
snowshoes, spreading their
weight and supporting them
on soft snow.*

THE GLUTTON
The wolverine is only the size of
a small dog, yet it kills reindeer by
chasing them into snowdrifts and
inflicting a crippling bite to the neck
as they flounder. This ferocious
animal has a huge appetite, but
even a wolverine can't eat a whole
reindeer. It hides the leftovers in
snow to freeze for eating later.

Stoats are immensely strong for their size. They can kill rabbits ten times their weight and haul them back to the den.

Despite its name, the fisher eats very few fish. It much prefers small mammals, eggs, and insects.

Snakes make up a small part of mongooses' diet. They mainly eat tiny animals like insects and spiders.

RABBIT CHARMER

The stoat charms its prey by leaping up and down in a bewitching dance. Rabbits become transfixed by this performance and sit still to watch it, unaware that the cunning stoat is inching slowly closer. When near enough, the stoat springs on the rabbit and bites into the victim's neck.

THE FASCINATING FOSSA

If you're ever lucky enough to see a fossa scampering down a tree, you might think you're watching a mutant cat with double-jointed legs. While cats struggle down tree trunks backwards, Madagascar's fossas can run headfirst by twisting their back feet round. Their agility allows them to race through the treetops while chasing Madagascar's other unique tree-dwellers, the lemurs.

FAST AND AGILE

Speed and agility are what save mongooses from a deadly bite when they hunt venomous snakes, such as the Indian cobra. By taunting the snake and darting from side to side, the mongoose eventually gets close enough to snatch it by the neck and crush its spine. Mongooses are not immune to snake venom, but they can survive a dose that would kill many other animals. As well as tackling poisonous snakes, they eat scorpions after biting off their stings.

CHEMICAL WEAPONS

Skunks are among the few mammals that defend themselves with chemical weapons. If a skunk fails to scare off an attacker by charging, stamping its feet, or performing a handstand, it plays its trump card: it turns round, lifts its tail, and fires a blast of foul-smelling liquid from nozzles flanking the anus. Skunks have a surprisingly good aim and can hit an enemy directly in the eye, causing intense pain and temporary blindness. People can smell the potent odour from up to 1 km (0.5 miles) away.

RODENTS AND RABBITS

A REMARKABLY SIMPLE INVENTION – self-sharpening teeth – has helped to make rodents and rabbits the most successful mammals on Earth. Rodents alone include some 2,000 species, accounting for nearly half of all mammals. They vary from the thinnest mice to sheep-sized capybaras, which can be as heavy as a man. Rodents can run, swim, climb, glide, hop, burrow, and leap, and they have conquered almost every conceivable habitat on land, including deserts, rainforests, the frozen arctic, and, of course, our cities and homes, where they live as pests. Rabbits and hares are similar to rodents, except for a slight difference in the teeth. They also have shorter tails and longer ears and legs.

LIFE WITHOUT WATER
Jerboas have adapted to life in the desert. They can manufacture water from food by a chemical reaction inside the body, so they never have to drink. In the heat of the day, jerboas hide in cool burrows. At night, they hop around like miniature kangaroos, looking for food.

ON THE RUN
Rabbits and hares are built for speed and have long hind legs for bounding. Because they feed in the open, they are always alert for danger. Eyes on the sides of the head give them all-round vision, and their long ears can pick up the quietest footsteps. Hares have longer legs than rabbits and are faster runners. Another difference is that rabbits raise their young in burrows, while hares hide them on the ground.

Hares can reach 72 kph (45 mph) as they try to outrun their pursuers.

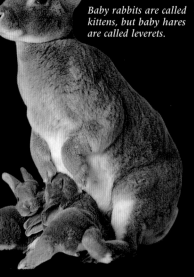

Baby rabbits are called kittens, but baby hares are called leverets.

BREEDING LIKE RABBITS
Rodents, rabbits, and hares are prolific breeders. Each year, a female rabbit can have six litters of up to 12 young, producing a maximum of 72 babies. When food is scarce, rabbits can slow down their furious rate of breeding by reabsorbing babies before they are born.

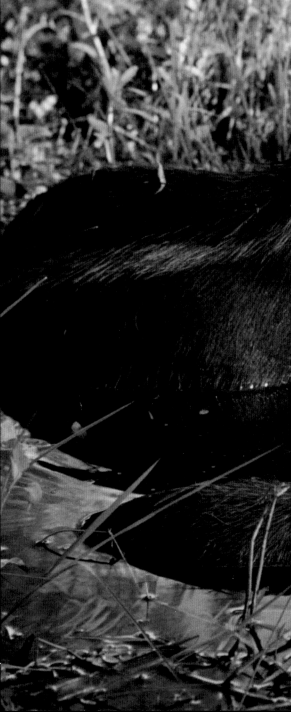

Pikas defend their territory by standing on rocks and squeaking.

HAY MAKERS
Pikas look more like guinea pigs than rabbits, but scientists place them in the same category as rabbits and hares. They live in high mountain meadows and are so used to cold weather that they die if it gets too warm. In autumn, pikas collect mouthfuls of grass and build a haystack to use during winter.

RODENT GIANTS

The capybara of South America is the giant of the rodent world, weighing up to 66 kg (146 lb) – about 10,000 times heavier than the smallest mouse. It lives partly in water and has eyes on the top of its head to see while swimming. Like other grass-eating rodents and rabbits, capybaras rely on symbiotic bacteria to digest their food. Because these bacteria live in the rear part of their intestines, capybaras have to eat their own droppings to get the most out of their food.

The harvest mouse has tiny, grasping hands and a long, gripping tail for climbing. It lives in a ball-shaped nest of woven grass blades, slung between grass stalks.

AGILE CLIMBERS

One of the smallest rodents is the Eurasian harvest mouse, which is a mere 5 cm (2 in) long (not counting the tail). It lives in tall grass, climbing between the stalks like a tiny monkey as it hunts for insects and seeds. Like many other rodents, harvest mice eat their own babies if food is in short supply.

GNAWING TEETH

At the front of a rodent's mouth are two pairs of incisor teeth that never stop growing. The front of each tooth is made of hard-wearing enamel, but at the back is a softer material called dentine. As a result, when the teeth rub together they wear the leading edge into a chisel-like blade, which is perfect for gnawing through the toughest nuts and seeds.

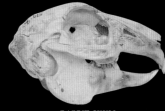

Rabbits have an extra pair of tiny peg teeth behind the incisors.

RABBIT SKULL

A gap between the front and rear teeth allows shavings to fall out of the mouth during feeding.

HAMSTER SKULL

Hamsters have huge cheek pouches that they stuff with food to carry back to the nest.

HAMSTER

HOMES AND SHELTERS

SMALL MAMMALS FACE LOTS OF CHALLENGES, but two of the greatest are keeping warm and not being eaten. A neat way of dealing with both is to build a snug shelter in which to hide, raise young, and sleep. An underground burrow is the most obvious solution, but some mammals are even more inventive. Bamboo bats squeeze into hollow bamboo stems, and North American flying squirrels make edible nests out of lichen. Beavers even build their own private island. In winter, when finding food gets especially difficult, some mammals stay in their hideaways for months on end, entering a kind of deep sleep called hibernation.

A BEAVER'S LODGE

Beavers live in an artificial island called a lodge, made from a mound of mud and sticks close to a dam. Inside the lodge is a spacious living chamber above the level of the water. Underwater tunnels allow the beaver to come and go without being seen, even when the pond freezes over. In winter, the beaver feeds on a stash of leafy branches gathered earlier in the year and kept chilled in the bottom of the pond.

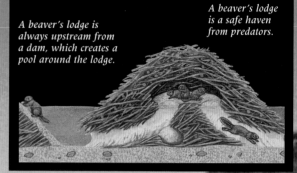

A beaver's lodge is always upstream from a dam, which creates a pool around the lodge.

A beaver's lodge is a safe haven from predators.

DAM BUILDERS

Beavers create artificial ponds and lakes by building dams across streams. Using their chisel-like teeth to cut trees to pieces, they pile thousands of stick and logs across the stream until it forms a watertight dam up to 90 m (300 ft) long, sealed with mud and rocks. Beavers slowly enlarge their dams year after year.

TEMPORARILY DEAD

A hibernating dormouse is so cold and motionless in winter that it seems to be temporarily dead. Its body temperature plummets to just one degree above freezing, and its heartbeat and breathing slow to less than a tenth of the usual rate. Dormice can stay like this for seven months.

During their long hibernation, dormice occasionally wake up for a few minutes.

Tent-making bats sleep under leaves during the day and wake up to feed at night.

TENT-MAKING BATS

Home for a tent-making bat is a folded leaf. These bats bite through the ribs of giant leaves to make them fold into a tent shape. Then they fly underneath and hang upside-down, protected from the rain and the eyes of predators. There are several species of tent-making bat in the rainforests of South and Central America, but the Honduran white bat is the only one with fur as white as snow.

UNDERGROUND CITIES

Prairie dogs live in vast burrow systems called towns, with interconnected tunnels providing a maze of routes to escape from predators. One of the biggest ever towns was reported to have 400 million residents and covered nearly a tenth of the state of Texas. Prairie dogs have now been exterminated in much of the American prairies because their burrows used to trip up horses and cattle, and break their legs.

WORM HUNTER

The European mole finds food by scurrying along its tunnels and catching any worms that fall in. When it finds a worm, it paralyses it with a venomous bite, squeezes the soil out of the worm's gut, and eats it. Moles can crawl forwards as well as backwards, and have whiskers at both ends for feeling in the dark.

Spare worms are stored in an underground larder.

Moles collect straw from above ground to build a warm nest.

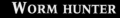

A mole has gigantic forelimbs for digging but tiny, almost useless eyes.

A single mole can build hundreds of metres of tunnels during its four-year life. Most of the tunnels run horizontally, but occasionally the mole digs a vertical shaft to get rid of the soil, pushing it out and creating a molehill.

ENDURANCE

THERE ARE FEW PLACES ON EARTH that mammals have failed to conquer, from the peaks of the highest mountains to the depths of the oceans. For mountain dwellers and polar animals, subzero temperatures are not the only hardship they have to endure. They also have to contend with air so thin that it would kill humans, or winters so harsh that food is impossible to find. In deserts, stifling heat and lack of water add to the challenge of finding scarce food. Ocean mammals face a very different endurance test: holding their breath. For, like all mammals, they have to breathe air, which they can only do at the surface.

SNOW MONKEYS
To beat the winter blues, Japanese macaques relax in a hot bath. The hot volcanic springs provide a welcome relief from winter temperatures as low as –15°C (5°F), though the monkeys can get a nasty chill when they climb out again and wait for their wet fur to dry out. Japanese macaques are the ultimate endurance monkeys and survive further north than any other monkeys, thanks partly to their luxuriously thick fur. In winter, when food is hard to find, they make do on a diet of bark and tree buds.

LIFE IN THIN AIR

High in the Andes, the air is so thin that mountaineers without oxygen tanks risk a deadly condition called altitude sickness. Yet vicuñas live comfortably at 4,000 m (13,000 ft). They survive in the thin air because they have unusually small, oval-shaped blood cells that efficiently absorb sufficient oxygen.

DEEP-SEA DIVER

As well as having the largest brain known to science, the sperm whale makes the deepest dives of any creature. It holds its breath for more than an hour as it plummets up to 3.2 km (2 miles) down to search for squid (in pitch darkness).

Sperm whales slow their hearts down and store oxygen in their muscles during their record-breaking dives.

Camels can lose up to half their body weight after a long spell without food or water.

SHIP OF THE DESERT

Camels can go for up to ten months in the desert without water, but how do they do it? Firstly, they can release water from food or from the store of fat in their hump. Secondly, when they do drink they can take in up to 136 litres (30 gallons) in one go, which is about a whole bathful, or a quarter of a camel's body weight. Thirdly, camels waste very little water in their sweat, urine, or faeces. Their droppings are so dry that desert people use them as firewood.

KEEPING YOUR COOL

Staying cool in the Sahara isn't easy. The fennec fox hides in its burrow during the heat of the day and keeps cool by panting up to 700 times a minute. Its enormous ears work like cooling radiators, helping it shed excess heat without having to sweat. Like many other desert animals, the fennec gets all its moisture from food and never has to drink.

The fennec's ears not only keep it cool, but also help it hear the faint sounds of its prey as it hunts at night.

COLOUR AND CAMOUFLAGE

ALL WILD ANIMALS LEAD LIVES OF CONTINUAL DANGER, and mammals are no exception. For most, staying out of sight is the first line of defence, so their fur coats are camouflaged – coloured or patterned to merge with the background. Most mammals are shades of brown, but many have beautiful stripes, spots, or rings to blend with grass or dappled shade. A few change colour to match the seasons. While the majority try not to be seen, some do the opposite: they sport shocking colours especially to attract attention.

BLACK AND WHITE
Polar bears have black skin but snowy white fur – perfect camouflage for sneaking up on seals. The fur is white because the hairs are hollow and transparent, making them scatter light. In sunny zoos, polar bears can turn green because algae grow inside the hairs.

ALBINO APE
Mammals get their colour from the chemical melanin, which is in the eyes, skin, and hair. In a few rare individuals, the genes that make melanin don't work properly. The result is an albino – a completely white animal. Most albinos are blind.

"Snowflake" the albino gorilla lives in Barcelona Zoo.

WHITE IN WINTER
Arctic foxes are brown in summer for camouflage in meadows. In winter, they turn white. Weasels, lemmings, and showshoe hares do the same. The trigger that makes them change is the number of hours of daylight. When the days get shorter, the brain releases a hormone that changes the fur colour.

BLACK PANTHER
The opposite of an albino is an animal with too much melanin. Black panthers are actually leopards, but they have so much melanin that their coats turn a glossy black. They are most common in dark forests. In the jungles of Malaysia, half the leopards are black panthers.

FLASHY FACES

The male mandrill has the most colourful face of any mammal, with a scarlet nose flanked by blue ridges, white whiskers, and an orange beard. Enormous, naked blue buttocks complete the look. Mandrills have brilliant colours simply because females prefer it that way. Over hundreds of generations, female preference has made the males ever more gaudy.

ATTENTION SEEKERS

For the first three months of life, silvered leaf monkeys are a startling orange colour. Then they turn a greyish black. Exactly why these monkeys have orange babies is something of a mystery. Scientists think the bright colour may be a signal to adults, triggering protective feelings while the infants are vulnerable.

LEOPARD   WILD BOAR PIGLETS   ZEBRA

HYENA   GIRAFFE   TIGER

SPOTS AND STRIPES

Spots and stripes can help to camouflage animals and break up their outline, but this isn't their only purpose. Zebras' stripes are hopeless as camouflage – they are much too conspicuous. They probably help zebras to recognize each other and bond with the herd.

INSECT EATERS

INSECTS CAN MAKE A RICH DIET – but only if you catch enough of them. While many mammals eat the odd grub, some have turned catching insects into a way of life. They come from a range of mammal families, but have evolved some striking parallels. The biggest specialize in raiding ant and termite nests. They have powerful claws for digging and long, sticky tongues. Smaller insect eaters, like shrews and tarsiers, use a different strategy. They have keen senses and lightning reflexes to catch their prey one at a time.

THE GIANT ANTEATER
The element of surprise is vital to South America's giant anteater. It can only steal about 100 ants and grubs from a nest before the colony's biting soldiers flood out. After tearing a hole with its huge claws, the anteater inserts its 60-cm- (2-ft-) long, sticky tongue, which darts in and out 150 times a minute, hooking prey with tiny, backward-pointing spikes. Giant anteaters visit up to 200 ants' nests a day, but they do very little damage to any of them.

Giant anteaters have been known to crush jaguars with their immensely powerful arms.

DIGGING FOR DINNER

With ears like a rabbit's and a snout like a pig's, the aardvark is one of the oddest animals in Africa. At night, it snuffles about in grasslands, sucking up soil into its snout and feeling for ants or termites. When it finds them, it digs into the nest and gathers ants with a tongue as sticky as flypaper. Aardvarks dig so quickly that they can disappear underground in just five minutes.

MAKING TRACKS

The elephant shrew has a miniature version of an elephant's trunk – a long and flexible snout, which it uses to sniff out ants, termites, beetles, and centipedes in Africa's savanna. It finds insects while darting nervously about a system of trails as complex as London's roads. It spends about a third of each day meticulously cleaning its trails, removing any twig or leaf that might trip it up when it needs to flee from danger.

ARMOUR PLATING

Pangolins have a long, sticky tongue to feed from ant and termite nests in the same way as anteaters. Sometimes they raise their scaly armour and let the angry ants scurry over their skin. The ants rid the skin of fleas and ticks that pangolins can't scratch.

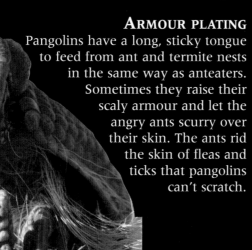

A three-banded armadillo rolls up to leave no openings for a predator to get to its soft parts.

Tarsiers' eyes are bigger than their brains. They have the biggest eyes, relative to body size, of any mammal.

Moths and flies are snatched from mid-air.

HAVING A BALL

Self-defence is important for armadillos because they often attract attention while rummaging about noisily for insects. Rolling into an armour-plated ball is the usual technique, but some can also escape danger by walking into rivers and holding their breath on the riverbed. Ants, termites, and beetles make up most of the diet. One species also burrows under rotting carcasses to gorge itself on maggots.

SLEIGHT OF HAND

With huge hands and quick reflexes, the tarsiers of Southeast Asia can snatch flying insects from mid-air. These nocturnal hunters can't move their eyeballs, so instead they swivel their heads right round, like owls. Moths, grasshoppers, beetles, and cicadas are their favourite food, but they also hunt lizards and baby birds. Sometimes they leap through the canopy to pounce on victims.

ON THE WING

WHILE BIRDS RULE THE SKIES DURING THE DAY, flying mammals take over at night. Various mammals have taken to the air, but the most famous and the most common are the bats. Though seldom seen, they make up a quarter of all mammal species and live all over the world. They are true fliers, with beating wings to keep themselves aloft. Other "flying" mammals are merely gliders. They leap off trees, stretch out their legs, and cruise through the air on a parachute of skin.

FLYING SQUIRRELS

America's flying squirrels can cruise 100 m (330 ft) between trees by gliding on flaps of skin between their legs. They steer by adjusting their feet and tails, and they brake by swinging the body upright. They lose height as they glide, so they have to scamper back up a tree before flying off again.

LIVING KITE

The colugo of Southeast Asia looks like a kite as it glides. Its furry gliding membrane stretches from the tips of its fingers to the tip of its tail. It is so huge and floppy that the animal is clumsy on its feet and almost helpless on the ground.

Babies cling tightly to the mother's stomach, while the mother's furry cloak forms a warm hammock for the baby.

For extra protection from predators, the colugos' fur is speckled for camouflage on lichen-covered branches.

Colugos are also called flying lemurs, though they aren't lemurs and they can't truly fly.

FRUIT BATS

Fruit and nectar make up the diet of the fruit bats – large bats that live in the rainforests of Africa, Asia, and Australia. They search for food at night, but unlike insect-eating bats, they have big eyes and find food by sight. They can cover 65 km (40 miles) in a night and island-hop their way across the vast Indian Ocean.

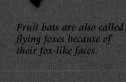

Fruit bats are also called flying foxes because of their fox-like faces.

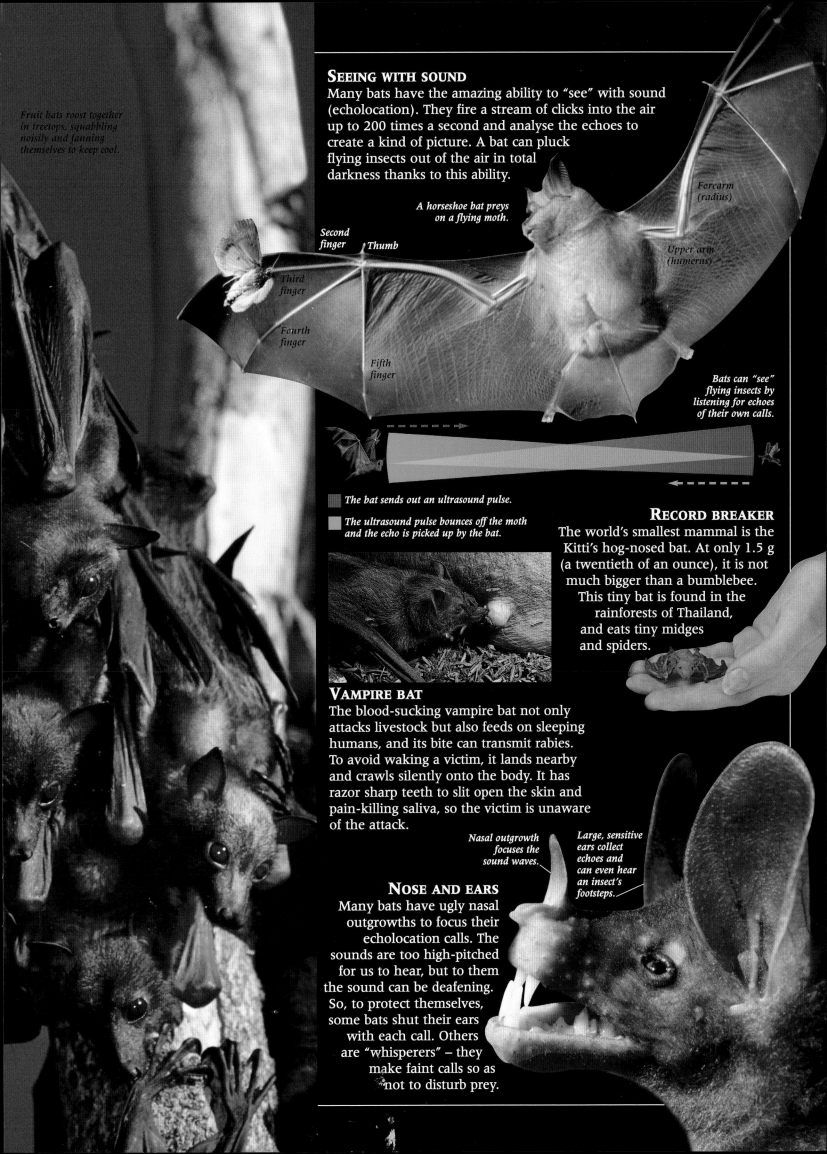

SEEING WITH SOUND
Many bats have the amazing ability to "see" with sound (echolocation). They fire a stream of clicks into the air up to 200 times a second and analyse the echoes to create a kind of picture. A bat can pluck flying insects out of the air in total darkness thanks to this ability.

Fruit bats roost together in treetops, squabbling noisily and fanning themselves to keep cool.

A horseshoe bat preys on a flying moth.

Forearm (radius)

Upper arm (humerus)

Second finger

Thumb

Third finger

Fourth finger

Fifth finger

Bats can "see" flying insects by listening for echoes of their own calls.

▮ The bat sends out an ultrasound pulse.

▯ The ultrasound pulse bounces off the moth and the echo is picked up by the bat.

RECORD BREAKER
The world's smallest mammal is the Kitti's hog-nosed bat. At only 1.5 g (a twentieth of an ounce), it is not much bigger than a bumblebee. This tiny bat is found in the rainforests of Thailand, and eats tiny midges and spiders.

VAMPIRE BAT
The blood-sucking vampire bat not only attacks livestock but also feeds on sleeping humans, and its bite can transmit rabies. To avoid waking a victim, it lands nearby and crawls silently onto the body. It has razor sharp teeth to slit open the skin and pain-killing saliva, so the victim is unaware of the attack.

Nasal outgrowth focuses the sound waves.

Large, sensitive ears collect echoes and can even hear an insect's footsteps.

NOSE AND EARS
Many bats have ugly nasal outgrowths to focus their echolocation calls. The sounds are too high-pitched for us to hear, but to them the sound can be deafening. So, to protect themselves, some bats shut their ears with each call. Others are "whisperers" – they make faint calls so as not to disturb prey.

LIFE IN WATER

WHILE MANY MAMMALS go for an occasional swim to forage for food or bathe, others take to water on a more regular basis. These amphibious mammals lead double lives, split between land and water. Hippos, for instance, come onto land only to feed, and return to water to rest. Seals and sea lions do the opposite. Over thousands of years, species that spend a great deal of time in water evolve bodies suited to their aquatic habitat. Their shape becomes streamlined, their fur becomes dense and velvety, and their legs eventually turn into flippers.

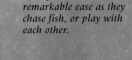

Sea lions twist and turn through the water with remarkable ease as they chase fish, or play with each other.

RIVER OTTERS

River otters have only partly evolved into aquatic animals. Their lithe and slender bodies, typical of the weasel family, give them amazing agility in the water, yet they can still scamper about and hunt on land. To keep them warm in water, otters have dense fur that traps a layer of insulating air.

Each square centimetre of an otter's coat contains 70,000 hairs.

SEA LIONS

Sea lions have gone further than otters in adapting to life in water. Their legs have become flippers, though they can still use them to support their weight and "walk" on land. Like otters, sea lions have dense velvety fur, but they also have a layer of blubber under the skin for extra insulation.

Sea lions use their sensitive whiskers to find the way in murky water.

Male elephant seals have a large inflatable snout to impress females.

ELEPHANT SEAL

Seals are even more aquatic than sea lions. Their outer ears have disappeared to make them more streamlined, and their flippers are almost useless on land – instead of walking they have to shuffle on their bellies. The elephant seal is the champion diver of the seal world. It can hold its breath for two hours and dive 1.5 km (1 mile) deep.

WATER SHREW

The water shrew holds its breath for more than 30 seconds as it dives for insects, frogs, and fish. Its long toes have a fringe of stiff hairs to give extra force to its kicks when it swims. This system works so well that the shrew can even run across the surface of the water for several metres without falling in. Its fine fur does the same job as an otter's, trapping a layer of air to keep the animal warm.

AQUATIC ACROBAT

Though slow and clumsy on land, seals and sea lions become swift and graceful as soon as they get in the water. Their swimming techniques are quite different. Sea lions propel themselves with powerful strokes of their strong front flippers, while using the hind flippers to steer. In contrast, seals swing their hind flippers sideways for propulsion and use the front flippers to steer.

SWIMMING TRUNKS

With their trunks serving as snorkels, elephants make such good swimmers that some scientists think they must have passed through an aquatic phase in their evolution. While African elephants only immerse themselves to bathe, Asian elephants are much more ambitious. In the Indian Ocean, working elephants sometimes swim for miles between the Andaman Islands, with their owners riding on their backs. A captive elephant once swam 64 km (40 miles) after falling off a boat en route to a zoo in the USA.

BLUSHING WALRUSES

Walruses have so much blubber that they risk overheating when they come out of the water to rest. So to shed excess heat, they blush – blood rushes to the surface of the skin and makes them turn pink. Walruses live around the edge of the Arctic Ocean, and have enormous, blubbery bodies for coping with the chilly water. They feed on the sea floor, grubbing around like pigs for crabs and shellfish hidden in the mud.

OCEAN GIANTS

WHALES, DOLPHINS, AND SEA COWS are the most aquatic mammals of all. Their four-legged ancestors left the land to live in water maybe 50 million years ago, beginning a process that changed them beyond recognition. Over time, evolution turned forelimbs into flippers, added a wide fluke to the tail, and made the hind limbs and fur wither away to nothing. With water to support their weight, some of these animals grew to monstrous proportions. All now spend their whole lives in water, though they come to the surface to breathe air. They eat, sleep, mate, give birth, and suckle their young entirely in water. If they ever leave the water, they risk crushing themselves to death.

Blue whales seem to find their way through the oceans by making deep booming noises and listening to the echoes that rebound off continents and the sea floor.

HUMPBACK WHALE

Leaping out of the water and letting its 30-tonne (27-ton) body crash back in is one of the ways that humpback whales communicate. To the highly sensitive ears of other whales, the splash must sound like a deafening explosion. Hearing is the most important sense for whales and dolphins. They use sound to locate food, to find their way, and to sing to each other over great distances.

Male humpback whales leap from the water and fall back on their sides. This spectacular display is called breaching.

BLUE WHALE

At 27 m (90 ft) long and 150 tonnes (136 tons) in weight, the blue whale is the largest animal ever to have existed. It is 33 times the weight of an elephant and one-and-a-half times heavier than the biggest dinosaur. Its tongue alone is the size of a car. Even in the coldest water, a blue whale's sheer size helps it retain heat.

TOOTHED WHALES

Scientists divide whales and dolphins into two major categories: toothed whales and baleen whales. The toothed whales include dolphins, porpoises, killer whales, and several other types of whale. All of them are intelligent predators, with sharp, peg-like teeth for snatching slippery prey like fish and squid. Killer whales even leap onto beaches to grab sea lions.

BALEEN WHALES

The largest whales are baleen whales. Instead of teeth, their mouths contain hundreds of bristle-covered "baleen plates" that hang from the upper jaw, forming an enormous curtain. Baleen whales feed by taking in a huge mouthful of water and forcing it through the baleen plates with the tongue. In each gulp, small animals like krill are sieved out of the water by the million.

Dolphins live in social groups called pods. They often swim in formation and leap out of the water together.

DOLPHINS

With a sleek, streamlined build, dolphins are built for speed in water. Though playful and friendly, dolphins also have a vicious streak – the males especially are often covered with the scars of battle. Like other toothed whales, dolphins hunt by echolocation. They make a stream of high-pitched sounds and their brains decipher the echoes to create a kind of picture.

KRILL

SEA COWS

Dugong and manatees are sometimes called sea cows because they are large, docile herbivores. They live in shallow water in the tropics – manatees in rivers and coasts around the Atlantic, and dugongs around the coast of the Indian and Pacific Oceans. Scientists think dugongs and manatees evolved from a land animal related to elephants. Whales and dolphins, on the other hand, probably evolved from a relative of the hippopotamus.

Dugongs grub about on the sea floor for the roots of an aquatic plant called sea grass.

MARSUPIALS

WHEN EXPLORERS brought the first opossum to Europe in the 16th century, the king of Spain in wonder put his finger in its pouch. Scholars called the pouch a "marsupium", meaning purse, and so this mammal group became known as the marsupials. In fact, not all marsupials have a pouch, but most do give birth to tiny babies that develop outside the mother's body. Most marsupials live on the islands of Australia, New Guinea, and Tasmania, but around 70 species of opossums live in the Americas.

LARGE LITTERS
Opossums can give birth to dozens of babies at once. The mouse opossum has no pouch, so its babies have to cling tightly to the mother, with their tails coiled around hers. At birth they are no bigger than rice grains. They quickly latch onto the mother's nipples, which fit in their mouths like plugs to hold them in place. If there are more babies than nipples, the spare ones drop off and die.

TINY TERRORS
Mulgaras look like cute mice, but in fact are vicious little carnivores. They eat house mice – from head to tail – peeling back the skin like a banana as they devour the flesh. They also like insects, centipedes, lizards, and birds.

BOXING KANGAROOS
In the mating season, male kangaroos battle for the right to mate. Standing upright, they lock their arms together and try to push their opponent over, or kick them in the belly. A lot is at stake in these fights – the victor gets to mate with all the females in the area, while the loser has to wait at least another year for a chance to mate.

During a fight, their immensely powerful hind legs slash at each other's belly.

MARSUPIAL MOLE

Some marsupials have evolved into counterparts of their nonmarsupial cousins, a process known as convergent evolution. The marsupial mole looks just like an ordinary mole, with huge claws for digging, a shovel-shaped head, and tiny, useless eyes. Unlike true moles, however, it doesn't dig proper burrows – instead it "swims" through sandy soil, which caves in behind it. Its pouch opens backward to prevent it filling with soil.

REPRODUCTION

The main difference between marsupials and placental mammals is the way they reproduce. Marsupials give birth to a tiny, underdeveloped baby that usually completes its development in a pouch. In placental mammals, the baby stays inside the uterus (womb) for much longer, attached to the mother by a placenta. While placental mammals have a single uterus and vagina, marsupials have a double system.

STRANGE DIETS

When a baby koala is old enough to stop suckling, its first meal is a mouthful of faeces from its mother's anus. The faeces contain vital bacteria, which live inside the koala's intestine and help it digest its normal food: eucalyptus leaves. Koalas are the only mammals that can live off eucalyptus leaves. The leaves are so low in nutrients and difficult to digest that koalas have to spend about 19 hours a day sleeping.

UTERUS 1 · UTERUS 2 · VAGINA 2 · VAGINA 1 · BIRTH CANAL

Kangaroos and wallabies often have an embryo "on hold" in the uterus while the pouch is occupied.

The nipple fills the mouth of a newborn kangaroo and holds it in place. This baby red kangaroo is about four weeks old.

RED KANGAROO

RED-NECKED WALLABY

The ears of Tasmanian devils turn bright red when they are angry.

Tasmanian devils have a very sharp sense of smell for sniffing out carrion.

TASMANIAN DEVIL

Though little bigger than a domestic cat, the Tasmanian devil is the world's biggest marsupial carnivore. It has immensely powerful jaws for crushing bones – which it then swallows. Tasmanian devils eat every scrap of a carcass including bones, fur, and feet. They also attack farm animals and are hated by Tasmania's farmers.

TAMING THE BEAST

ANIMALS THAT ARE BOTH CLEVER AND SOCIABLE – as many mammals are – can easily learn to live with humans. For thousands of years, people have domesticated all sorts of mammals, carefully breeding them to make them tamer and more useful: horses became taller and faster than their wild ancestors, dogs shrank and grew friendlier, while pigs, cattle, and sheep got fatter, more docile, and more stupid. Domestication also transformed our own species, triggering the beginnings of agriculture, city life, and civilization. Today, the mammals we keep have countless uses – we eat them, milk them, ride them, make clothing from them, train them to hunt and work for us, and keep them as pets.

NORTH
AMERICA

Guinea pig (3,000 years ago)

SOUTH AMERICA

Llama (7,000 years ago)

MAN'S BEST FRIEND

The ancestor of the domestic dog was the grey wolf. Today, most dog breeds look very different from wolves, but their behaviour gives them away. Just like wolves, they are pack animals that form strong social bonds. Well-trained dogs see humans as the leader of the pack, which is why dogs are so friendly and obedient. Dogs are useful in lots of ways: as pets, hunting companions, guards, sniffer dogs, and for pulling sleds across snow.

Huskies still bear a strong resemblance to grey wolves, their distant ancestors.

Herding cattle is an important way of life in tropical grasslands, where the weather is too harsh for crops.

MEAT, MILK, AND BLOOD

Cattle are descended from a wild animal called the aurochs, which is now extinct. People once hunted herds of aurochs, but over time they learnt to lead and drive the animals. Today, cattle are kept for milk as well as meat. The Masai people of Africa also drink the blood, taking a little at a time from a vein in the cow's neck.

The map shows approximately where and when people began to keep various domestic mammals. Many of the dates and locations are uncertain.

Cattle (8,000 years ago)

Horse (6,000 years ago)

Goat (9,000 years ago)

EUROPE

ASIA

Pig (8,000 years ago)

Dog (15,000 years ago)

Camel (5,000 years ago)

Cat (5,000 years ago)

AFRICA

AUSTRALIA

ANTARCTICA

DOMESTICATION DATES

The first mammal to be domesticated was probably the dog, perhaps as early as 15,000 years ago in China. Between 9,000 and 6,000 years ago, the people of Western Asia invented agriculture and domesticated many of the farm animals that we keep to this day. South America's people invented agriculture separately and domesticated a range of very different mammals.

LIVING TRACTORS

In Asia, people use water buffaloes instead of tractors to plough marshy fields before sowing rice. Like their wild, swamp-dwelling ancestors, domestic water buffaloes have splayed feet for walking on mud, and they often spend the heat of the day wallowing in water. When the animals reach the end of their working lives, their owners eat them.

BEAST OF BURDEN

Llamas and alpacas are domestic versions of the wild guanacos and vicuñas that live in the high Andes mountains of South America. They are valued as much for their thick wool as for their strength as beasts of burden. They are close relatives of camels, and, like their cousins in Africa, they can withstand extreme environments, such as deserts and mountains.

Working elephants use their trunks to move heavy logs. A mahout – the elephant's owner and driver – sits on its neck.

WORKING ELEPHANTS

Elephants are among the few animals able to fell whole trees, an ability that made them invaluable to Asia's timber industry. In recent times the timber industry has gone into decline, but working elephants are still to be seen carrying tourists around wildlife reserves, or taking part in religious festivals.

57

URBAN LIVING

HIDING IN OUR GARDENS AND UNDER OUR FLOORBOARDS are all sorts of mammals that have adapted to city life. From house mice to urban moose, these animals have discovered that humans are wasteful and messy creatures with an unending supply of food. Some urban mammals are occasional visitors – they raid our dustbins, eat our gardens, or break into our homes to steal pet food and kitchen scraps. Others are permanent residents, benefiting from central heating and shelter from the weather. Most of these squatters and thieves are adaptable omnivores – they like the same kind of food as us, which means our leftovers are full of rich pickings.

URBAN MOOSE
Believe it or not, Anchorage in Alaska has a population of more than 1,000 urban moose. These giant deer spend most of their time in the greener parts of town – such as people's gardens – munching on shrubs and trees. Like forest-dwelling moose, they like water and sometimes immerse themselves in ponds or paddling pools for a rest.

THE MASKED BANDIT
The raccoon's nickname – the masked bandit – is well earned. Raccoons not only push over dustbins to get into them, but can break into houses by climbing through windows and crawling through cat-flaps. Their dexterous little hands, normally used for feeling about in rivers for shellfish, are perfect for opening plastic packets and paper bags. Raccoons also flip over newly laid turf to pull out the worms.

CITY SLICKER

An overgrown garden or a crevice under a shed make a perfect den for the red fox, a cunning and adaptable animal that has spread all over the world. Urban foxes live in the cities of North America, Europe, and Australia, but they are seldom seen because they stay out of sight in daylight hours. While rural foxes eat small animals, worms, and berries, their urban cousins make do with the contents of dustbins. Their favourite food is leftover meat, but they also like bread, potato peel, bird seed, and eggs.

MAN'S WORST FRIENDS

Brown rats thrive in sewers and feed on the rubbish we drop on the streets or flush down the drain. As true omnivores, they eat everything from plants and seeds to rotting meat, slugs, wax, insects, soap, cardboard, hair, fingernail clippings, and any animal too small to bite back. They also spread disease, including the bubonic plague that killed 25 million Europeans in medieval times.

Red foxes can smell what's in a dustbin before looking. Like raccoons, they push over bins to knock the lids off. They also tear open plastic rubbish bags with their teeth.

PARTY ANIMALS

Vervet monkeys are native to Africa, but in the 17th century they found their way to the Caribbean island of St Kitts on slave ships. Rum production was the island's main industry, and the monkeys soon acquired a taste for alcohol. Today they raid beach bars and tourist resorts for drinks.

Hanuman langur monkeys get free handouts of petals and fruit at temples devoted to the god Hanuman.

SACRED MONKEYS

In India, followers of the Hindu religion view certain animals as sacred and allow them to run freely about towns and temples. The Hanuman langur monkey, for instance, is named after the Hindu god Hanuman. In many Indian cities, sacred cows wander the streets without harm, and at one temple in India, worshippers come to feed a plague of holy rats.

WEIRD AND WONDERFUL

WHEN SCIENTISTS IN ENGLAND FIRST SAW A PLATYPUS – a dried skin sent from Australia – they declared it a fake. It seemed too weird to be true, as though stitched together from bits of other animals. Yet the platypus turned out not only to be real, but also to have a way of life even stranger than its anatomy. Two hundred years later, we now know that the world is full of weird and wonderful mammals. Of the 4,600 or so mammal species that exist, no two are exactly alike. Each has solved the challenge of surviving in its own unique way.

The babirusa's upper tusks form from canine teeth in the top jaw that grow upwards instead of downwards.

BABIRUSA

The babirusa of Southeast Asia has tusks that grow straight up through its snout and out of the skin. Only males have these painful looking tusks, so they probably serve to impress females. When males fight, they bash their heads together and try to snap each other's tusks off.

An extraordinary bill and huge webbed feet make the platypus look like a cross between a beaver and a duck.

PLATYPUS

As well as being one of the few mammals that lays eggs, the platypus is the only one with a poisonous sting. Even stranger, its duck-like bill can sense electricity. When the platypus swims, it shuts its eyes and uses the bill (like a metal detector) to scan the riverbed for electric fields made by prey.

LION OR TIGER?

When closely related species breed together, they sometimes produce peculiar offspring called hybrids. A liger is the offspring of a male lion and a female tiger. It has a mixture of the parents' features but is much bigger and stronger, though unable to breed. One captive liger in the USA is more than twice the weight of a male lion, making it the world's largest cat.

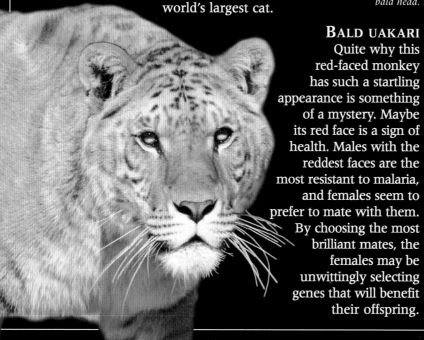

The bald uakari has a scarlet face and a completely bald head.

BALD UAKARI

Quite why this red-faced monkey has such a startling appearance is something of a mystery. Maybe its red face is a sign of health. Males with the reddest faces are the most resistant to malaria, and females seem to prefer to mate with them. By choosing the most brilliant mates, the females may be unwittingly selecting genes that will benefit their offspring.

PYGMY MARMOSET

The world's smallest monkey is the pygmy marmoset of the Amazon rainforest. Barely larger than a gerbil, it runs along branches rather than clambering between them as other monkeys do. It feeds by gnawing holes in trees and sipping sap, and after a meal it urinates on the site to keep other marmosets away.

Pygmy marmosets are small enough to perch on the thinnest twigs.

A Virginia opossum can play dead for up to six hours.

PLAYING POSSUM

When a Virginia opossum is cornered, it "plays possum". It pretends to be dead by falling on its side and going into a kind of trance that slows its heart and breathing rate. For extra realism, it releases a foul-smelling slime from its anus to mimic the stench of decay.

Instead of grasping branches, sloths hang below them with their hook-like claws.

STAR-NOSED MOLE

A set of 22 wriggling tentacles on the nose of this mole gives it one of the most peculiar sense organs in the mammal world. The star-nosed mole uses its amazingly sensitive nose to feel for small animals in soil and underwater. Unlike most moles, it is an expert swimmer and can use its huge front feet either as diggers in soil or paddles in water.

SLOTH

The sloths of South America move so slowly that they seem to live in slow motion. Their diet of leaves is very low in nutrition, so sloths conserve all the energy they can. They sleep most of the day and defecate only once a week always descending a tree to do so. A sloth is a walking ecosystem. Its dank fur is stained green by algae and inhabited by a mass of ticks, moths, and beetles.

MAMMAL DATA

EVOLUTION OF MAMMALS

Scientists have identified more than 4,680 species of mammals. Together they make up the class Mammalia. Over 200 million years ago the class separated into the mammals that laid eggs (monotremes) and those that gave birth to live young (subclass Theria). Later, there was a further split of subclass Theria into marsupials and placental mammals.

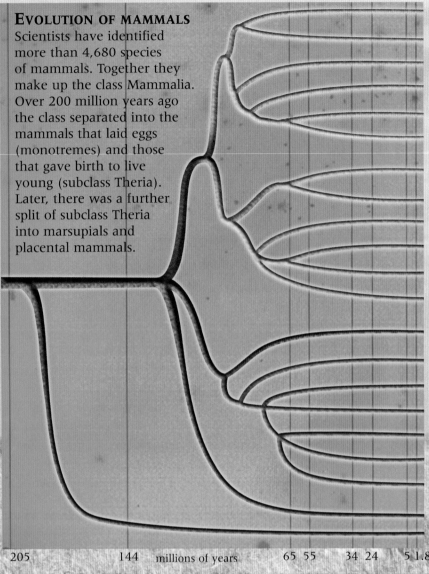

Rodents (order Rodentia) 1,999 species

Rabbits, hares, pikas (order Lagomorpha) 87 species

Tree shrews (order Scandentia) 18 species

Shrews, moles, hedgehogs (order Eulipotyphla part of order Insectivora) 399 species

Colugos (order Dermoptera) 2 species

Primates (order Primates) 256 species

Pangolins (order Pholidota) 7 species

Carnivores (orders Carnivora and Pinnipedia) 264 species

Odd-toed ungulates (order Perissodactyla) 16 species

Even-toed ungulates (order Artiodactyla) 196 species

Whales and dolphins (order Cetacea) 88 species

Bats (order Chiroptera) 977 species

Anteaters, sloths, armadillos (order Xenarthra) 29 species

Tenrecs and golden moles (order Afrosoricida part of order Insectivora) 45 species

Elephant shrews (order Macroscelidea) 15 species

Aardvark (order Tubulidentata) 1 species

Hyraxes (order Hyracoidea) 11 species

Dugong and manatees (order Sirenia) 4 species

Elephants (order Proboscidea) 3 species

Marsupials (7 orders) 289 species

Monotremes (order Monotremata) 3 species

205   144   millions of years   65 55   34 24   5 1.8

CRITICALLY ENDANGERED MAMMALS

The *2002 ICUN (International Union for the Conservation of Nature and Natural Resources) Red List of Threatened Species* names 181 mammals as critically endangered in the wild. This list includes:
Abyssinian wolf currently found in Ethiopia
Baiji (changjiang dolphin) currently found in Yangzte River, China
Black-faced lion tamarin currently found in Brazil
Cochito (vaquita porpoise) currently found in Gulf of California
Garrido's hutia currently found in Cuba
Kouprey (grey ox) currently found in Cambodia
Iberian lynx currently found in Portugal and Spain
Javan rhinoceros currently found in Indonesia and Vietnam

Malabar civet currently found in India
Mediterranean monk seal currently found in Atlantic Ocean, Mediterranean Sea, and Black Sea
Northern hairy-nosed wombat currently found in Australia
Pygmy hog currently found in India
Seychelles sheath-tailed bat currently found in Seychelles
Sumatran rhinoceros currently found in Indonesia, Malaysia, Myanmar, Thailand, and Vietnam
Tamaraw (dwarf water buffalo) currently found in Philippines
Tonkin snub-nosed monkey currently found in Vietnam
Yellow-tailed woolly monkey currently found in Peru

GROWING OLD

The mammal with the shortest life span is the pygmy shrew, which lives a maximum of 13 months. Humans hold the record for the longest life span, of 120 years. Life spans are affected by lifestyles and the level of threat from predators.

MAXIMUM LIFE SPANS

Mouse 6 yrs	Rabbit 13 yrs	Dog 20 yrs	Tiger 26 yrs	Cow 30 yrs	Polar bear 38 yrs	Bison 40 yrs

GLOSSARY

Amphibious The ability to move or live both in water and on land.

Aquatic Living in water.

Blubber A thick layer of insulating fat that forms the skin of sea mammals and polar bears.

Camouflage A pattern, colour, or body shape that helps an animal hide by blending in with its surroundings.

Carnivore An animal that eats flesh. Also, a member of the mammalian order Carnivora.

Convergent evolution The independent evolution of similar features in different animals, such as wings in bats and birds.

Echolocation Seeing by sound. Bats and dolphins echolocate by producing special sounds and analysing the echoes.

Herbivore An animal that mainly eats plant food.

Hibernation A type of very deep sleep in which an animal's body systems almost shut down to help it conserve energy.

Marsupial A type of mammal that gives birth to tiny young that develop further in a pouch, or attached to teats on the mother's belly.

Migration A long journey undertaken by animals to find food or a place to breed. Many animals migrate each year during certain seasons.

Monotreme A type of mammal that lays eggs.

Nocturnal Active at night.

Omnivore An animal that eats both plant foods and animals.

Placenta An internal organ that allows unborn mammals to absorb food and oxygen from the mother's bloodstream.

Primate A type of mammal with grasping hands, forward-facing eyes, and a large brain.

Prosimian A type of primate that is only distantly related to monkeys and apes. Most are small nocturnal creatures.

Rainforest A type of forest that gets heavy rain all year round. Tropical rainforests occur in tropical parts of the world; temperate rainforests occur in cooler places.

Rodent A type of mammal with sharp, chisel-like front teeth for gnawing.

Rumination Regurgitating food to chew it a second time. Ruminant animals have a special stomach containing bacteria that help them digest plant food.

Savanna Areas of grassland found in tropical regions.

Symbiosis A very close relationship between two different species.

Warm-blooded Having a relatively constant internal body temperature.

MAMMAL RECORDS

Biggest marine mammal Blue whale. Largest recorded length: 33.5 m (110 ft). Largest recorded weight: 196 tonnes (193 tons). Bigger examples may exist.

Biggest land mammal African elephant. Largest recorded length: 7.3 m (24 ft); height: 4 m (13 ft); weight: 14.9 tonnes (13.5 tons).

Tallest mammal Giraffe. Tallest recorded length: 6 m (20 ft).

Smallest mammal Bumblebee (Kitti's hog-nosed) bat. Head and body length: 27.9–33 mm (1.1–1.3 in).

Fastest land mammal Cheetah. Fastest speed recorded: 105 kph (65 mph).

Slowest land mammal Three-toed sloth. Speed in trees: 0.27 kph (0.17 mph).

Largest litter Common tenrec. Largest number recorded: 32 (30 survived), although normal litter size is 15.

Longest gestation period Indian elephant. Average period of 609 days (over 20 months) with a maximum period of 760 days (22 months).

Shortest gestation period American opossum (Virginian opossum) and rare water opossum (yapok). Average period of 12–13 days.

Longest migration (swimming) Grey whale. A round trip of 20,000 km (12,400 miles).

Deepest diver Sperm whale. Can probably reach depths of at least 3.2 km (2 miles).

Highest altitude Yak. Can climb to about 6,000 m (20,000 ft).

Loudest land mammal Howler monkey. Sound can be heard 4.8 km (3 miles) away.

Loudest sound produced Some baleen whales produce sounds that can travel all the way across entire oceans. The sound of blue whales and fin whales have been recorded at 188 decibels.

Smelliest mammal Striped skunk. Its smell contains seven major volatile and foul-smelling chemicals.

MAMMAL WEBSITES

Rhino	Chimp	Hippo	Dolphin	Indian elephant
50 yrs	53 yrs	54 yrs	65 yrs	77 yrs

INDEX

ACKNOWLEDGMENTS

Dorling Kindersley would like to thank the following people for their help with this book: Andrew O'Brien for original digital artworks; Chris Bernstein for compiling the index; Simon Holland for editorial assistance; Karl Stange for DK Picture Library research.

Dorling Kindersley would also like to thank the following for their kind permission to reproduce their photographs:

Key:
c = centre; l = left; r = right; b = bottom; t = top

Inside book credits:

alamy.com: Bryan & Cherry Alexander Photography 34tr, 44tl, 56c; Noella Ballenger 32cr; Steve Bloom Images 1c, 5ca, 16bl, 20c, 23c, 32bl, 34cl, 53cl; Bruce Coleman Brakefield 45bl; Mike Hill 38tr; ImageState 45bc; ImageState /

D. Robert Franz 17br; ImageState / Mike Hill 7b; ImageState / Jan Tove Johansson 54r; Leo Keeler 30crb; Photos for Africa / Johan Jooste 23br; Pictures Colour Library 21br; Malie Rich-Griffith 7c; Royal Geographical Society / Martha Holmes 6c; Stock Connection Inc. / John W. Warden 31br; Worldwide Picture Library 57c; **Ardea London Ltd:** Ian Beames 41tl; J. Cancalosi 38bl; Jean-Paul Ferrero 7cr; M.W. Gillam 55tl; Pascal Goetgheluck 36b; Francois Gohier 52c; Nick Gordon 47cr; Clem Haagner 47tl; Chris Harvey 8c; Masahiro Iijima 57br; Chris Knights 38cl; Pat Morris 7tr; D.Parer and E. Parer-Cook 53tr; Jagdeep Rajput 59br; Wolshead / Ben Osborne 57tr; **Steve Bloom / stevebloom.com:** 22b, 28r, 29t; **Bruce Coleman Ltd:** 55bl; Johnny Johnson 40bl, 51br; Luiz Claudio Marigo 60br; Rinie Van Meurs 53br; Jim Watt 50bl; Jorg and Petra Wegner 30br; **Bruce Coleman Inc:** Wolfgang Bayer 61br;

Corbis: Yann Arthus-Bertrand 21tl, 21tc, 21tr; Tom Brakefield 15cl, 37br, 46c, 60bl; W. Perry Conway 28cl, 36l; Cordaiy Photo Library / John Farmer 29b; D. Robert and Lorri Franz 36tr; Rose Hartman 40c; Gallo Images 28bl; Nigel J.Dennis 32cl; Clem Haagner 13c; Martin Harvey 55bc; Renee Lynn 16br; Gunter Marx Photography 30br; Joe McDonald 5tr, 61c; Kevin Schafer 13br; Ariel Skelley 4cl; Paul A. Souders 42tr; Jim Zuckerman 22l; **FLPA - Images of nature:** Lynwood Chase 61bl; Michael Guinton 29cl, 29c, 29cr; Frans Lanting 37tr; Minden Pictures: Mitsuaki Iwago 9br, 11bl, Frans Lanting 19br, 47br, S. Maslowski 7tl, T De Roy 25tr; Mark Newman 11tr; Eddie Schuiling 9c; Silvestris fotoservice 54cl; **Getty Images:** 24br; Thea Allats 48r; Daniel J. Cox 27cl, 55tr; Tim Davis 16tl; John Dawner 8tr; Chris Johns 18tl; David W. Hamilton 2c; G.K. and Vikki Hart 18b; National Geographic: Skip Brown 8tr, Beverly Joubert 26br, Bates Littlehales 41cr; Mitch Reardon 20tr; Kevin Schafer 27c; Anup Shah 26bl; Manaj Shah 16tr, 16b; Taxi 10r; Joseph Van Os 42c; Art Wolfe 26tr; **ImageState / Pictor:** Natural selection

Inc 44br; **Nature Picture Library:** Juan Manuel Borrero 44bl; Wendy Darke 51r; Bruce Davidson 17c; John Downer 12c, 47tr, 58cr; Tony Heald 25br; Brian Lightfoot 37tc; Dietmar Nill 49tr; Mark Payne-Gill 47cl; TJ Rich 29ca; Jeff Rotman 18r; Anup Shah 15br, 17bl, 19cr, 24bc; John Waters 39l; Mike Wilkes 39tr; **N.H.P.A.:** 5c; B and C Alexander 24c; Anthony Bannister 43bl; Joe Blossom 60tl; Stephen Dalton 58r; Manfred Danegger 41br; Nigel J Dennis 34b; Martin Harvey 4tr; Daniel Heuclin 7cr; Rich Kirchner 33c; T. Kitchin and V. Hurst 30cl, 58bl; David and Irene Myers 53cr; Steve Robinson 43br; Andy Rouse 61l; Kevin Schafer 41tr; James Warwick 5cra; Dave Watts 15tl, 60c; **Oxford Scientific Films:** 19cr, 21cr, 49cl; AA: Zig Leszczynski 15r, Patti Murray 35tr; Kathie Atkinson 9cr, 54bl; David W. Breed 22ca; Clive Bromhall 11cr; David Cayless 43c; Waina Cheng 48bl; David Haring 12tr; Chris Knights 38ca, 38car; Lon E Lauber 58cl; Okapia: B. Grizmek 15br; J.L. Klein and M.L. Hubert 39tr, 16b; Taxi 10r; Stan Osolinski 45l; Mike Powles 5tl; Alan Root 10bl; SAL / Mike Price 56bl;

Keren Su 31cr; Steve Turner 55br; **Powerstock:** 19tr; Mirko Stelzner 13tr; **Seapics.com:** 43tc; Phillip Colla 52tr; Doug Perrine 35tr; **Science Photo Library:** Art Wolfe 45tr; **Still Pictures:** Klein / Hubert 44tr; **Zefa Picture Library:** T. Allofs 50r; H. Heintges 50br; K. Schafer 14c.

Jacket credits:

Front: Alamy / Royal Geographical Society. Back: Alamy / Steve Bloom Images (cr), Alamy / Bruce Coleman Brakefield (r), Alamy / Worldwide Picture Library (cl); Back and spine: Getty Images / Anup Shah (r).

All other images:

© Dorling Kindersley. For further information, see www.dkimages.com

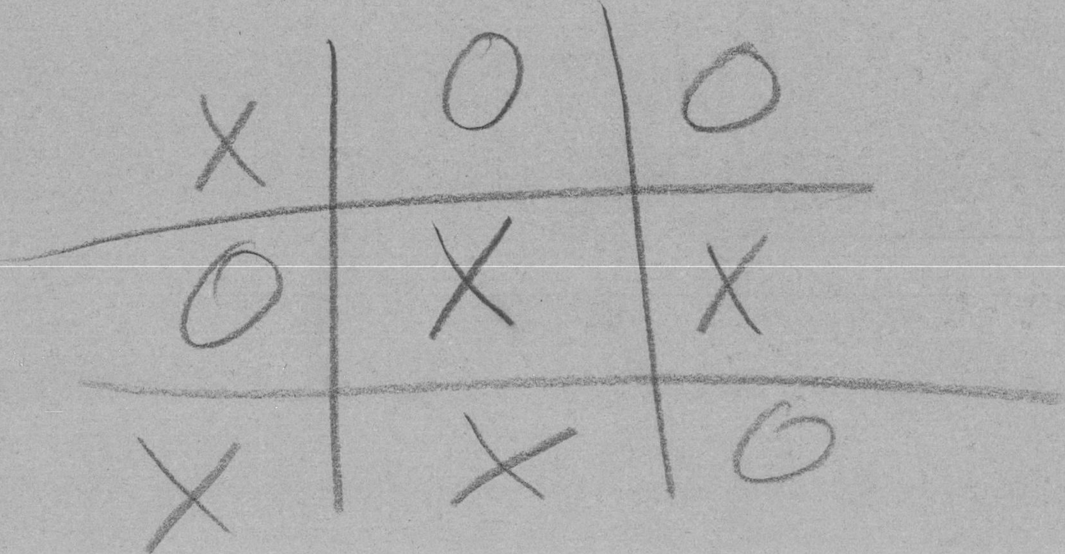

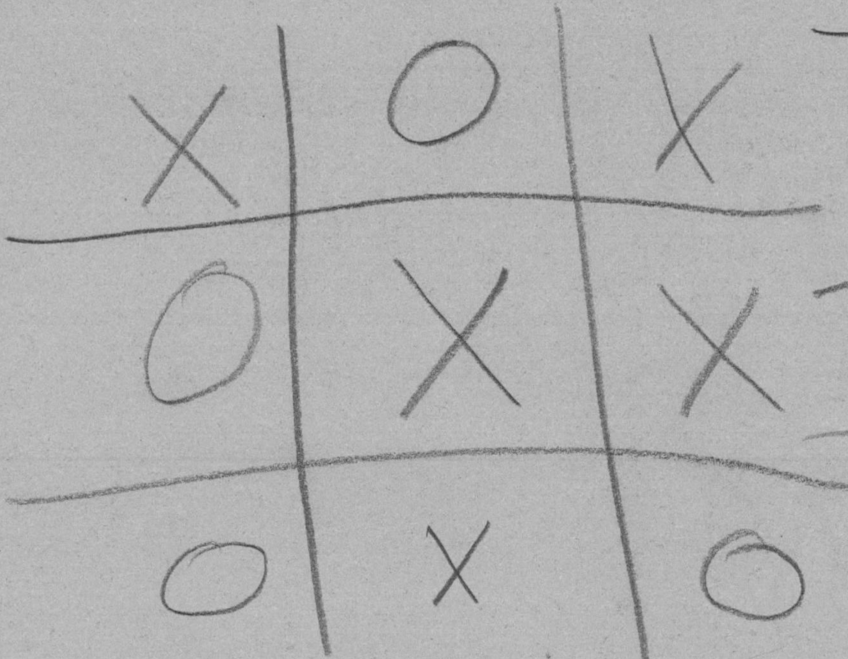

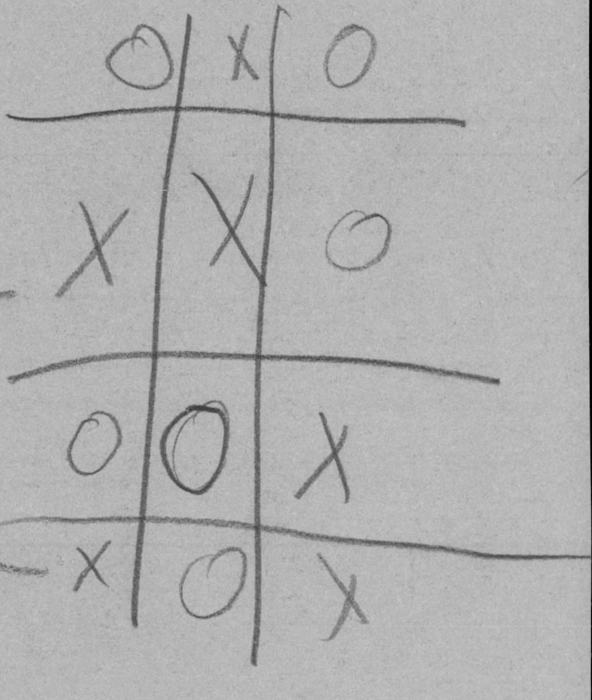

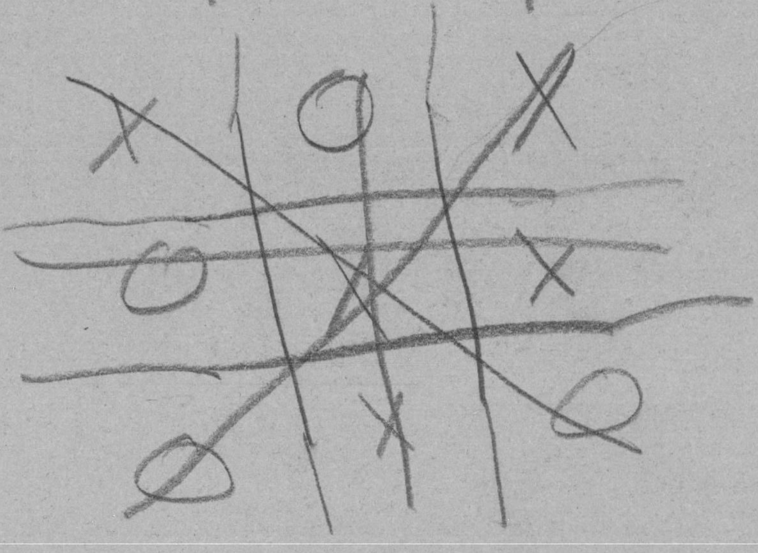